THE PASSIONATE PURSUIT OF GOD
LESSONS FROM THE BOOK OF PSALMS

CENTRE FOR PENTECOSTAL THEOLOGY
BIBLE STUDY SERIES

Edited by
Lee Roy Martin
John Christopher Thomas

CPT Press
Cleveland, Tennessee

THE

PASSIONATE
PURSUIT OF GOD

LESSONS FROM THE BOOK OF PSALMS

Lee Roy Martin

CPT Press
Cleveland, Tennessee

Handouts and PowerPoint presentations may be downloaded free of charge at http.//pentecostaltheology.org under 'Resources'.

The Passionate Pursuit of God
Lessons from the Book of Psalms

Centre for Pentecostal Theology Bible Study Series

Published by CPT Press
900 Walker ST NE
Cleveland, TN 37311
USA
email. cptpress@pentecostaltheology.org
website. www.cptpress.com

ISBN-13: 9781953358332

Cover art by Gerard van Honthorst – 'King David Playing the Harp' (1622)

This book is dedicated to
my fellow pastors
who have taught and encouraged me over the years.

TABLE OF CONTENTS

PREFACE

The title of this book is based on the frequent expressions of deep passion in the Psalms – passionate prayer and passionate praise, ultimately, the passionate pursuit of God. Note, for example, the passionate longing for God expressed in Psalm 42.1-2:

As the deer pants for the water brooks,
So pants my soul for You, O God.
My soul thirsts for God, for the living God.
When shall I come and appear before God? (NKJV)[1]

The passions of the Psalms came to my attention when, as a student at Lee College, I read through the entire Bible for the first time. Therefore, my own pursuit of God's presence and God's anointing was fueled by the Psalms. Furthermore, I discovered that the passions of the psalmist were mirrored in the writings of great spiritual leaders such as Martin Luther, John Wesley, George Whitefield, Charles Finney, E.M. Bounds, and Leonard Ravenhill.

My serious study of the book of Psalms began in 1993, when I was called upon by Lee University to teach an undergraduate course on the Psalms. As part of my preparation for the course, I read Claus Westermann's important work, which led me to conclude that the passionate emotive content of the Psalms should be explored more fully. Furthermore, I was convinced that the passions expressed in the Psalms were an appropriate point of entry for a Pentecostal approach to the Psalter ('Psalter' is another name for the book of Psalms). I was reading Westermann's *The Living Psalms* as I sat in the Chattanooga Convention Center, waiting for the Tennessee Camp Meeting service to start. At that moment, the outline for this book came to my mind, and I recorded it in the front of my Thompson Chain-Reference Bible. Now, almost thirty years later, that outline has become a book.

---

[1] All quotations of Scripture are from the New King James Version unless designated otherwise.

My idea for writing on the Psalms was put on hold when I began to teach at the seminary; and I found myself working day and night while pastoring a church, teaching at the seminary, writing a doctoral thesis, and raising a family. Reflecting back on my choices, though, I cannot explain why I never considered the Psalms as a doctoral project. All I can say is that there is a time and a season for all things; and apparently, 1993 was not the time for me to write on the Psalms.

My interest in the Psalms was renewed in 2010, when I re-read Psalm 1; and the word 'delight' (v. 2) leaped out at me. The verse reads, 'His delight is in the law of the LORD, and in his law he meditates day and night'. At that moment, I realized that the Holy Spirit was showing me something different from what I had read in the commentaries. Affected by the word 'delight', I saw the law as a source of joy rather than as a duty. Instead of a demand for obedience, I saw Psalm 1 as an invitation to a life of blessing. My hearing of Ps. 1.2 prompted me to spend the next eight years researching and writing on the book of Psalms.

This book expounds on nine different psalms, and each psalm was chosen for a specific reason. I began with Psalm 1 because of its role as an introduction to the Psalter. Psalm 13 was chosen because it is a psalm of prayer (what scholars call 'lament'). Out of the 150 psalms, more than 60 are lament psalms. I included Psalm 22 because of its use by Jesus Christ on the cross. Psalm 27 is a psalm of trust and has been a favorite of mine for many years. Psalm 30 represents the psalms of testimony, in which the psalmist praises God for an answered prayer. Psalm 51 is one of the most famous psalms, and it is a model for sincere confession and repentance. Psalm 63 is included because it expresses the passionate pursuit of God that underlies much of the Psalter and which is the heart of Pentecostal spirituality. I chose Psalm 73 because it stands at the center of the book of Psalms and because it teaches us how genuine worship addresses our deepest questions and concerns. Finally, Psalm 150 is the climax of the book of Psalms; and it reflects the ultimate goal of the Christian life – absolute praise of God.

I offer my thanks to the pastors in the Church of God who have used my Jonah Bible study and who have encouraged me to write more Bible studies that can be used in the local church. Also, this book would not have been possible without the support and endorsement of the administration at the Pentecostal Theological Seminary. President Michael Baker and Vice-President for Academics David Han have consistently encouraged faculty to create resources for Church of God ministers and laity.

I serve as the James W. Hamilton Professor of Teaching Lay Involvement; therefore, I also extend my gratitude to Jim Hamilton and to his wonderful family, whose vision for lay involvement initiated the faculty chair that provides partial funding for my work.

The support of my family is valuable beyond words. They give me more encouragement and affirmation than anyone deserves. I offer special thanks to my wife Karen for her keen editorial eye and for her willingness to use it to make me look like a skilled writer.

Psalms is a powerful book, and I trust that this study will encourage you to love the Lord and to pursue the Lord with all of your heart. 'Let everything that has breath praise the LORD' (Ps. 150.6).

Lee Roy Martin
Cleveland, Tennessee
August 27, 2022

HOW TO USE THIS BOOK

This Bible study is written for pastors and lay persons who desire to live a Spirit-filled life that is formed and directed by Holy Scripture. Although the book is presented in popular language, it is based upon an in-depth exegesis of the Psalms from the original Hebrew text.

This book is appropriate both for individual readers and for group study. Therefore, the materials are grouped into two parts. The Bible study can be enjoyed by individual readers, or it can be used in a group setting. Handouts and PowerPoint presentations are available for use in the group setting. They can be downloaded online at no charge. Go to http.//pentecostaltheology.org and look under the 'Resources' tab.

The study follows nine individual psalms. Each lesson includes quite a large amount of material. Therefore, although the course is divided into nine lessons, you may find it more practical to spread each lesson over two or more class sessions.

The lessons are presented in four steps that are based on the well-known 4MAT learning process (Meaning, Content, Experiment, Creative application).

Each step serves as a stage in the learning process, and each step also addresses the different learning styles of students. Step one is an introduction to the lesson and may include group discussion. Step two is the basic content of the Scripture lesson. Steps three and four bring the lesson to bear upon the Christian life, the church, and the world. These can be times of discussion that provide for more extensive student participation and interaction. The teacher should be at liberty to spend as much time as necessary on each step, depending upon the needs and desires of the students. Also, teachers are encouraged to create their own learning activities that are appropriate for the students and to their particular context.

The four learning steps may be described as follows.

1. Setting the Direction

The purpose of the first step is to stimulate student interest in the topic. In this step we answer the question, 'Why do we need to study this lesson?' Teachers can feel free to lead a discussion that brings to the surface the life needs of the students in relation to the lesson at hand. Initial discussions can be based upon the teacher's own context or upon the suggested Discussion Starters that are offered in the book. The overall goal is to involve the students and their personal testimonies so that they become deeply engaged in the topic at hand. The challenges faced by each student will resonate with other members of the group, and a sense of community will develop.

2. Hearing the Word of God

The second step is to present the basic Bible lesson, and it comprises the bulk of the material in this manual. Here we answer the question, 'What do we learn from this Scripture passage?' The lesson is presented according to a Wesleyan–Pentecostal approach to Scripture that recognizes the guidance of the Holy Spirit, the role of experience, the relationality of truth, and the importance of God's dealings with humanity (the story of Scripture). Thus, the Bible is more than a roadmap or list of principles; instead, it is God's living, dynamic Word that continues to speak to God's people in new and creative ways.

3. Connecting with Psalms

The purpose of the third step is to apply the Scripture to our churches and to our lives as Christians. We answer the question, 'How does this lesson pertain to us?' In this step, we submit our lives to the Holy Spirit. We must be open to the convicting power of the Holy Spirit, who will challenge, confront, and transform the believer who is hungry for God and willing to hear God's voice. The goal of Bible study includes not just the acquisition of information, but the acknowledgment that each of us is held accountable for what we hear in Scripture.

4. What if ... ?

This final step is a creative process that seeks to answer the question, 'How can we build upon the foundation laid in this lesson?' In other words, the lesson serves as a base for generating new and imaginative ideas that move beyond the basic applications that are discovered in step three. How do we live in the presence of God? How do we demonstrate the love of God to the world? In light of our Bible lesson, what is God calling us to do?

For more information on teaching with the students' learning styles in mind, see Marlene D. Lefever, *Learning Styles: Reaching Everyone God Gave You to Teach* (Colorado Springs, CO: David C. Cook, 2002).

UNDERSTANDING THE BOOK OF PSALMS

The book of Psalms is sometimes referred to as the songbook of Israel, and both Jews and Christians have consistently witnessed to the power of the Psalms to give voice to their prayers and their expressions of worship. The Psalms have this power because, unlike other parts of Scripture, they are not God's words directed towards Israel. Rather, the Psalms are Israel's words directed to God in worshipful and prayerful response to his presence and actions among them. As long as Christians continue to acknowledge God's presence and activity in the church, the Psalms will serve as a meaningful expression of the Christian response to God in worship and prayer. The Psalms provide examples of prayer and worship, and they have much to say about our worship today.

The Psalms are lyric poetry and exhibit all of the features of poetry. The 150 Psalms were written by a variety of Hebrew authors over the span of several hundred years. The Psalms include several types of songs that vary considerably in style, content, and form. The Psalms are cited often in the New Testament, where many of them are associated with the life of Jesus the Messiah. The importance of the Psalms is illustrated further by their continued use throughout history, both in public worship and in private devotions.

What are the Psalms?

Songs of Worship
The Psalms tell us that worship is deep, intense, and passionate. Worship flows out of the believer's relationship with God. Psalm 23 tells us that we can experience God in *personal relationship*: 'The Lord is my shepherd'. Yes, God is the great shepherd of the church, but as the

psalmist declares, he is 'my' shepherd. As my shepherd, the Lord provides for my needs. As my shepherd, the Lord brings me to the green pastures where I can find rest. As my shepherd, the Lord leads me to a place of refreshing beside the still waters. As my shepherd, the Lord 'restores my soul'. When I walk in the dark valley, I do not fear because my shepherd walks with me to protect me. He strikes out with his rod against any enemy that might approach, and he stretches forth his staff to guide me and to pull me closer to himself. Because the Lord is my shepherd, I will worship him.

The Psalms tell us also that prayer is honest and fervent. In fact, the Psalms' honesty and fervency may at times seem harsh, especially on those occasions when the psalmist prayed for the violent destruction of enemies and their children (e.g. Ps. 3.7). These imprecatory psalms are difficult to reconcile with Christ's command to love our enemies. It should be remembered, however, that these psalms are cries for help, emerging from situations of deep suffering and oppression, and that the New Testament allows for God's intervention as vindicator of his people (Rom. 12.19; 1 Thess. 1.8; 2 Tim. 4.14; Heb. 10.30-31; Jude 14-15; Rev. 6.10).

A Collection of Songs

Psalms is a collection of songs that were brought together over a period of hundreds of years, beginning with a collection of David's psalms, with others added later. Psalm 137, for example, was written after the Babylonian captivity, several hundred years after the time of David. Psalm 137 remembers the days when the Israelites were in the land of Babylon and the Babylonians asked them to sing a song from the land of Israel, but the Israelites hung their harps on the willows. That was about 500 BC, and David had lived about 1000 BC – a span of 500 years. Over this period of five hundred years, the Psalms were compiled. Therefore, it is not a book like the other books of the Bible; instead, it is a collection of individual songs written by multiple song writers.

The Five Books of Psalms

The book of Psalms is divided into five divisions, which are called the 'Five Books':

Book One:	Psalms 1–41
Book Two:	Psalms 42–72

Book Three: Psalms 73–89
Book Four: Psalms 90–106
Book Five: Psalms 107–150.

The psalms in each of these five books were grouped together on account of similarities in topic, perspective, usage in worship, or authorship. Most of the psalms of David are in Books One and Two, but other psalms of David are scattered throughout the entire Psalter. The fivefold division of the Psalter may have been intended as a structural parallel to the five books of Moses.

The five books are marked off with a doxology that concludes sections 1, 2, 3, and 4. The doxologies are as follows:

'Blessed be the Lord God of Israel from everlasting to everlasting. Amen and amen' (Ps. 41.13).

'Blessed be his glorious name forever and ever. Let the whole earth be filled with his glory. Amen and amen' (Ps. 72.19).

'Blessed be the Lord forevermore. Amen' (Ps. 89.52).

'Blessed be the Lord God of Israel from everlasting to everlasting, and let all the people say, "Amen, praise the Lord"' (Ps. 106.48).

Thus, these sections end with similar declarations of praise to the Lord. These doxologies are like links, holding the book together.

Authorship of the Psalms

When we think of the book of Psalms, we naturally think of them as the Psalms of David, but not all of them were written by David. Even Psalm 1, the very first psalm in the book, does not include the heading, 'A Psalm of David'. Psalm 1, along with many other psalms, does not include the name of the writer. Still, among the psalms that give the name of the author, David is credited with writing 73. However, Moses is named as the author of Psalm 90; Solomon wrote Psalms 72 and 127; Heman wrote Psalm 88; Ethan wrote Psalm 89; a group called 'the sons of Korah' wrote eleven psalms (Pss. 42, 44-49, 84-85, 87-88); and another group called 'the sons of Asaph' wrote eleven Psalms (Pss. 73-83). The names of these authors are supplied in the headings of the psalms. The authorship of some fifty psalms remains unknown. Because David wrote more of the psalms than anyone else and because he is known as 'the sweet psalmist of Israel'

(2 Sam. 23.1), the whole book is sometimes given the name, 'The Psalms of David'.

Groupings of Psalms

In addition to the five books within the Psalter, here are several other groupings of Psalms. One group is called the pilgrimage songs or the songs of ascent. These are Psalms 120 through 134. The pilgrimage psalms were sung by the Jews when they traveled to Jerusalem for the great feast days – the Day of Passover, the Day of Pentecost, and the Day of Atonement. Another group is called the Hallel, or praise psalms (Psalms 113-118, 146-150), and they were sung during certain festivals (The Hebrew word *hallel* means 'praise'). For example, Psalms 113 through 118 were sung during the Feast of Tabernacles. Still another group is called the Elohim psalms (or the Elohistic Psalter). This group gets its name from the Hebrew word *Elohim*, which is one of the Old Testament's names for God. In the Hebrew Bible, there are several different names for God. *Elohim* is the general name that means 'God', and the Hebrew word *Yahweh* is the personal name of Israel's God. Yahweh is usually translated 'the Lord' or 'Jehovah'. In Psalms 1-41 and 84-150, the name *Yahweh* occurs much more often than the name *Elohim*. However, Psalms 42-83 almost always use the word *Elohim* rather than *Yahweh*; therefore, those psalms are called the Elohistic Psalter.

Different Types of Psalms

The book of Psalms is often characterized as a book of praises to the Lord. However, the very first psalm does not contain a single word of praise to God. We learn from the outset, therefore, that the book of Psalms contains songs of many different kinds. By employing a variety of psalm types, the Hebrew psalmists were able to respond in worship to the many different situations in their lives. Biblical scholars have identified five basic genres of psalms: the individual lament (prayer), the communal lament, the communal hymn, individual thanksgiving psalms, and royal psalms. Other scholars would also suggest categories such as wisdom psalms, psalms of Zion, historical psalms, and psalms of trust. These genres do not exhibit strict, ironclad structures, nor do they explain the nature of every song in the entire collection. Nevertheless, they are helpful guides to understanding the basic forms of biblical psalmic expression.

Throughout this book we will say more about the psalms of lament, hymns, thanksgiving psalms, wisdom psalms, and psalms of trust. Other, less common types of psalms include the following.

Creation Psalms

The creation psalms focus on praising God as creator. For example, we read in Psalm 19, 'The heavens declare the glory of God, and the firmament shows forth his handiwork' (v. 1). A vital point of Old Testament teaching is that God created all things (see Gen. 1.1; Isa. 40.38). Other songs of creation include Psalms 8, 19, 24, 33, 65, 104, and 148.

Royal Psalms

The royal psalms are psalms that celebrate the rule of God's chosen Davidic king. They also praise God as eternal king. God is the king of Israel, the world, and the universe. He is Lord. The royal psalms include Psalms 2, 18, 20, 21, 45, 72, 101, 110, 132, and 144.

Historical Psalms

In the historical psalms, the psalmist tells a portion of the history of Israel. Some of the historical psalms cover the story of Israel from the days of Abraham all the way up to the time when the psalm was written. Throughout these recitals of Israel's story, the psalms will praise God because he brought Israel out of Egypt and because he helped the patriarchs. These psalms, through their emphasis on God's faithfulness, provide encouragement to the Hebrew people. The historical psalms include Psalms 78 and 136.

The different kinds of Psalms teach us different aspects of worship. The presence of the wisdom psalms within Israel's song book suggests the importance of instruction as a part of worship. The songs of prayer demonstrate that biblical worship should provide a time and place for passionate prayer, for crying out to God. The songs of testimony demonstrate the value of telling our story to one another in the context of worship, praising God for specific acts of deliverance. The hymns teach us to praise God for his unchangeable attributes. They show us that the goal of worship is absolute praise.

The Psalms Are Written in Poetic Form

Poetry may be defined as a verbal composition that intensively expresses feelings and ideas through its choice of exalted language and its patterned arrangement of words and phrases.

Poetic Figurative Language

One important feature of typical poetry is the use of figurative, symbolic language. Figurative language is the symbolic use of words to convey a meaning that is different from the literal meaning. The book of Psalms is filled with figurative language. The psalmist declares, 'The Lord is my shepherd' (Ps. 23.1). However, David is not literally a 'sheep,' and God is not literally a 'shepherd'. The symbol of the Lord as shepherd communicates that he is provider, guide, and protector. Other examples of figurative language include the following:

'The Lord is my rock and my fortress' (2 Sam. 22.2)

'But I am a worm, and no man' (Ps. 22.6)

'Their throat is an open tomb' (Ps. 5.9)

'He is a shield to all who trust in Him' (Ps. 18.30).

The process for the purification of silver is used as symbolic language when the psalmist writes, 'The words of the LORD are pure words, like silver tried in a furnace of earth, purified seven times' (Ps. 12.6). Silver, in fact, is melted and filtered in order to remove any foreign elements. Silver that has been purified seven times is very, very pure. Similarly, the words of the Lord are very, very pure. There is nothing foreign or unclean in God's words.

We mentioned above that figures of speech add emphasis and get our attention. Sometimes this emphasis takes the form of an intentional and obvious exaggeration for the sake of making a point. For example, the psalmist describes the troubled mariners on the sea when their ship rides the stormy waves: 'They mount up to the heavens, They go down again to the depths' (Ps. 107.26). The words 'heaven' and 'depths' are symbols of the rise and fall of the gigantic waves as they lift the ship and then cause it to descend into the trough.

Because of his troubles, the psalmist often speaks of his grief and his weeping in exaggerated terms. His weeping is so profuse that he uses the symbolism of the 'flood' and the 'river'. For example, he writes, 'All night I make my bed swim; I drench my couch with my tears' (Ps. 6.6). Also, he says, 'Rivers of water run down from my eyes, Because people do not keep your law' Ps. 119.136).

Finally, God is described with figurative language by attributing to him a human form. As we know, God is a spirit (Jn 2.24) and does not possess a physical body. Describing the attributes of God can be difficult, because God is a spirit; therefore, the biblical writers sometimes use human forms as a means of illustrating God's characteristics. For example, biblical poets use the word 'hand' to signify the power of God. For example, David prays, 'Save with your right hand, and hear me' (Ps. 108.6). The Psalms also refer to God's 'ears'. David prays, 'Bow down your ear to me, deliver me speedily' (Ps. 31.2). The words, 'Bow down your ear to me', form a figure of speech through which David is asking for the Lord to hear his prayer. He is asking God to listen and to respond with the answer. In a few psalms, God is even described symbolically through reference to animal forms. For example, the psalmist speaks of God as if he has wings and feathers. He says, 'He shall cover you with His feathers, And under His wings you shall take refuge' (Ps. 91.4). The wings of God represent his protective covering which he spreads over his people.

Poetic Verse Structure

In the Psalms, a poetic verse may consist of one, two, or three lines, but most often it will be two lines, with the second line related in some fashion to the first line. The second line may restate the thought of the first line; it may state the antithesis of the first line; or it may complete the thought of the first line. Note the following examples:

> The heavens declare the glory of God;
> the skies proclaim the work of his hands (Ps. 19.1-2)

The second line repeats the same general idea using different terminology. 'Heavens' and 'skies' are synonyms, and 'declare' and 'proclaim' are synonyms. Another example is.

> Do not fret because of evildoers,
> Nor be envious of the workers of iniquity (Ps. 37.1)

In this case, 'fret' is synonymous with 'be envious,' and 'evildoers' is synonymous with 'workers of iniquity,'

The second line states the antithesis of the first line in Ps. 1.6:

> The Lord knows the way of the righteous,
>   but the way of the ungodly shall perish (Ps. 1.6)

The second line states a truth that is the counterpart to the first line and completes it. In this instance, 'the righteous' are opposite to 'the ungodly'; and the actions of the Lord in the first line are opposite to his actions in the second line. Another example is:

> For evildoers shall be cut off;
>   But those who wait on the Lord shall inherit the earth (Ps. 37.9)

Here we see that evildoers have a different end from those who wait upon the Lord.

There are still other kinds of connections between the first line and the second line of a Hebrew poetic verse. The second line may provide the reason for the first line; it may ask a question based upon the first line. The first line may be a comparison with the meaning of the comparison given in the second line. For example,

> As a father pities his children,
>   so the LORD pities those who fear him (Ps. 103.13)

Another structural technique is the acrostic poem, in which each verse begins with successive letters of the Hebrew alphabet (e.g. Psalms 25, 34, 111, 112, 119, and 145). Psalm 119 is unique in that it consists of 22 sections, one for each letter of the Hebrew alphabet; and every verse within a section begins with the same letter. In biblical times, the average believer did not possess a copy of the Scriptures. Therefore, it was important that people be able to memorize as much of the Bible as possible. Poetry was an aid to memorization, and acrostic poetry was even more easily remembered than standard poetry.

Experiencing the Psalms

It is hoped that this brief introduction to the Psalms will aid the reader in understanding the message that is found in these poignant prayers and powerful praises. The full richness of the Psalms can only be appreciated, however, when we move beyond analysis to experience. That is, the Psalms should not be seen as objects of study; rather, they should be seen as scenes of life. As we read a psalm, we should enter into its world, placing ourselves within its setting, its events, and its story. Let the words of the psalm be our words, expressing our thoughts, our feelings, and our relationship to God. Their inspiring use throughout the centuries has proven that the Psalms can serve as potent expressions of our prayers and our praises, our hopes, and our dreams. Therefore, the Psalms can help us to express our *Passionate Pursuit of God.*

1

THE PASSIONATE PURSUIT OF GOD'S WORD: PSALM 1

Setting the Direction

Happiness is a valued but illusive treasure. Everyone wants to be happy and content. Everyone is chasing after happiness. Yet, how do we achieve happiness? Where is happiness to be found? Does happiness come through material possessions? Does happiness come through personal success? Can we find happiness at the end of the rainbow? Is our happiness dependent upon others: our parents, our spouse, our children, our friends, or even our employer?

According to Scripture, the pursuit of happiness is equivalent to the pursuit of God. True happiness and genuine contentment occur only within the context of our covenant relationship with God. We are created in the image of God, and we are created to walk with God. We are 'His people and the sheep of His pasture' (Ps. 100.3). He has created us to be his people, a people who will 'show forth the praises of him who called us out of darkness and into his marvelous light' (1 Pet. 2.9).

We learn from Ps. 1.2 that real happiness comes to us only as we 'delight' in God's Word. Psalm 1 is an introduction to the book of Psalms, and it was put at the very beginning of the Psalter to teach us that if we intend to serve God joyfully, we must serve him out of a heart that is attuned to his Word. The happy person, the true worshiper, finds 'his delight' in the Word of God and in his Word he 'meditates day and night' (Ps. 1.2). To delight in the Word of God is to have it in our hearts, to love it, to take pleasure in it, and to rejoice in it.

Therefore, if we intend to study the Psalms, to read the Psalms, to pray the Psalms, to sing the Psalms, and to experience the Psalms, we must first examine our hearts. If we are interested only in listening to the advice of wicked people, then we cannot hear what God would to say to us. If we walk on the pathway with sinners, then we will not be able to walk with Jesus. If we sit with scorners and boasters and those that rebel against God, we will not submit ourselves to the law of the Lord. So this is where we begin our study of the Psalms – with the heart of the believer.

Discussion Starters

Describe your own search for happiness.

Explain how God's Word is a 'delight' to you.

How does reading the Bible contribute to our passionate pursuit of God?

Is it possible for a Christian to have a vibrant and living relationship with God?

The Apostle James wrote, 'Draw near to God, and He will draw near to you' (Jas 4.8). How does Jas 4.8 relate to our pursuit of God?

Hearing the Word of God

Psalm 1

¹ Blessed is the man
  Who walks not in the counsel of the ungodly,
  Nor stands in the path of sinners,
  Nor sits in the seat of the scornful;
² But his delight is in the law of the LORD,
  And in His law he meditates day and night.
³ He shall be like a tree Planted by the rivers of water,
  That brings forth its fruit in its season,
  Whose leaf also shall not wither;
  And whatever he does shall prosper.
⁴ The ungodly are not so,
  But are like the chaff which the wind drives away.
⁵ Therefore the ungodly shall not stand in the judgment,
  Nor sinners in the congregation of the righteous.
⁶ For the LORD knows the way of the righteous,
  But the way of the ungodly shall perish.

Introduction

Psalm 1 encourages us to passionately pursue God's Word. This encouragement is framed in terms of a contrast between the blessedness of the righteous person and the ruination that comes to the wicked person. The Psalm can be divided into two parts:

The Blessedness of the Righteous (vv. 1-3)
The Ruination of the Wicked (vv. 4-6).

The righteous person is not influenced by evil and does not practice evil but, instead, delights in the Word of the Lord and meditates in it. The person who delights in the Word of God is like a flourishing and productive tree.

The wicked, in contrast to the righteous, are like worthless husks of grain. The wicked person has no standing at the place of judgment and no place in the congregation of the righteous. The Psalm's overall theme of the blessedness of the righteous (expressed through the contrast between the righteous and the wicked) is confirmed and sharpened in the final verse – 'The LORD knows the way of the righteous, but the way of the wicked will perish'. It is the Lord's providence that guarantees the blessedness of the righteous and the destruction of the wicked.

The Righteous are Favored by God

Blessed is the man
Who walks not in the counsel of the ungodly,
Nor stands in the path of sinners,
Nor sits in the seat of the scornful; (Ps. 1.1)

Psalm 1 begins with words of affirmation: 'Blessed is the man…' The word 'blessed' is a translation of the Hebrew *asher*, which means 'fortunate', 'happy', or 'favored'. It refers to those who, because of their relationship to God and their walk with God, are living a blessed life. Psalm 1.1 carries an idea very similar to that of the beatitudes in Jesus' sermon on the mount: 'Blessed are the poor in spirit … Blessed are those who mourn … Blessed are the meek …', and so forth (Mt. 5.3-11). This happiness is a sense of well-being, of satisfaction, of being fortunate. Those who are blessed are flourishing, joyous, and satisfied with their lives. The blessedness of Psalm 1 is not accidental; it is given by God to those who walk in his ways and who love his Word.

The following examples illustrate the meaning of the word 'blessed' as found in Ps. 1.1.

'Behold, blessed is the man whom God corrects' (Job 5.17).

'Blessed are all those who put their trust in Him' (Ps. 2.12).

'Blessed is he whose transgression is forgiven, Whose sin is covered' (Ps. 32.1).

'Blessed is the man to whom the LORD does not impute iniquity, And in whose spirit there is no deceit' (Ps. 32.2).

'Blessed is the nation whose God is the LORD' (Ps. 33.12 and 144.14).

'Blessed is he who considers the poor' (Ps. 41.1).

'Blessed are those who dwell in Your house' (Ps. 84.4).

These verses help us to envision the deep and genuine happiness that accompanies those who seek after God and who give themselves in service to the needs of those around them.

The Righteous Follow the Right Path

Psalm 1 explains that in order to be truly happy and blessed we must not pursue evil. Again, verse 1 says,

Blessed is the man
Who walks not in the counsel of the ungodly,
    Nor stands in the path of sinners,
    Nor sits in the seat of the scornful; (Ps. 1.1)

The 'ungodly' are the *resha'im*, the 'wicked', whose behavior is evil. Their words and deeds are contrary to God's character and also are hostile to those who are around them. The behavior of the wicked shows that they are not in a right relationship to God. The words 'wicked' and 'righteous' are used as opposites in the Bible.

According to Ps. 1.1, the righteous person avoids three kinds of evil. First, the righteous do not listen to wicked counsel: 'Blessed is the man who does not walk in the counsel of the wicked'. What does it mean to walk in the counsel of the wicked? Our walk is our behavior; and counsel is advice, plans, ideas, opinions, or values. If we are righteous, we do not model ourselves after those who are wicked. When we start looking for a model for advice and counsel, we must be sure that we listen to the right people instead of listening to the wicked. The wicked will not give us the kind of advice that we need to hear.

Second, the righteous do not accompany sinners in their activities. We read, 'Blessed is the man who does not … stand in the path of sinners'. A sinner is a person who is disobedient to God and is not obeying God's commandments. The path of sinners is their way of life, and to stand in their path is to become a part of their way of life.

Third, the righteous do not 'sit in the seat of the scorners'. A scorner is a person who is a scoffer, who boasts and rebels against God's authority. For us to sit in the seat of the scoffer is to remain there and to make it a part of our surroundings. To sit there means that we acclimate to it, become a part of it, accommodate it, and assimilate the scornful attitude and way of life. Thus, the true worshipers are characterized in Ps. 1.1 first of all by what they do not do. They do not pursue evil; they are not interested in it, even though they may be tempted and tested.

Sometimes we may see wicked people who appear to be prospering, and they seem to have it all together. Apparently, they have everything they need and want, but we can see only the outward appearance. God, however, knows what is in the heart. The wicked do not possess genuine and lasting joy. Material prosperity is fleeting and cannot bring happiness. Those who are righteous do not pursue evil; but instead, the righteous person pursues the Word of God.

The Righteous Love the Word of God

After naming the evils that the righteous person avoids, the psalmist now turns to the positive attributes of the righteous. Blessed are those who do not pursue evil; but instead, their delight is in the law of the Lord. Verse 2 says,

> **But his delight is in the law of the LORD,**
> **And in His law he meditates day and night (Ps. 1.2).**

In this verse, the word 'law' does not mean a list of rules, regulations, orders, or commands. Instead, the Hebrew word for law is *Torah*, which means instruction or teaching. The whole of God's word is his Torah, his teaching, his instruction. In the Hebrew tradition, the Pentateuch, which consists of the five books of Moses, is also called the Torah.

Psalm 1 introduces the book of Psalms as a book of teaching and instruction. It is God's Torah (teaching) for us; and we should delight ourselves in it. Some Bible commentators have written that Psalm number one is all about obedience. They have said that a person must come to God in worship first as a duty or an obligation because it is something that God requires. However, the psalmist tells us that the righteous person *delights* in God's teaching. The righteous person loves God's teaching. The focus of Ps. 1.2 is not upon obligation or duty; instead, its focus is upon the affections of the heart. The righteous person loves God's Word, takes pleasure in it, and meditates in it. The Word of God is our passionate pursuit.

When we become a Christian, God changes our hearts. We are transformed by the power of the Gospel. The Apostle Paul writes, 'Therefore, if anyone is in Christ, he is a new creation; old things have passed away; behold, all things have become new' (2 Cor. 5.17). When we become Christians, our entire outlook changes; and our desires and affections are redirected. Instead of running *from* God, we run *to* God. Instead of avoiding the Word of God, we seek out the Word of God. Our hearts are attuned to God and to his Word. We are eager to spend time in prayer, and we long for deeper experiences of worship and praise.

Unfortunately, the initial joys of the Christian life are sometimes overshadowed by the passage of time; and our love for God is eroded by disappointments, pain, and heartbreaks. Real worship happens when we go back and renew our first love. In the book of Revelation, God tells the church at Ephesus, 'You have lost your first love' (Rev. 2.4). We may be doing everything we are supposed to do – we may be going to church, we may be praying, we may even read the Bible – but if we are only doing these things out of duty and obligation then there is something missing. We should have a desire, a passion in our hearts. We might compare our relationship to God with that of our spouse. Married people fall out of love, because they forget why they loved the person that they married; and they forget how to love that person. Their hearts begin to wander, and they forget about the person they love. Part of the importance of maintaining a good marriage is to always maintain a sense of delight in the spouse. Married people must maintain a desire to be with their partner. If that desire is lost, it must be regained or else the marriage will fail. Those who enjoy a long and happy marriage have learned how to nurture the love and delight for their spouse.

The righteous person delights in the Torah, the Law of the Lord. The word 'delight' has reference to the affections. It is defined as ' to take joy in,' 'to take pleasure in.' It denotes the direction of one's heart or passion,' a pleasurable emotional attraction. Outside the Psalter, 'delight' can denote the attraction between a man and a woman – we read that the son of Hamor 'delighted in Jacob's daughter' (Gen. 34.19). Also, 'delight' can refer to God's pleasure in his people and their actions – the Israelites are hopeful that Yahweh 'delights' in them (Num. 14.8), and Samuel insinuates that Yahweh has greater 'delight' in Saul's obedience than in his sacrifices (1 Sam. 15.22). The Lord takes pleasure in his people. He delights in saving the sinner; there is rejoicing in heaven when a person is converted (Lk. 15.7). We are his people; and he delights to see us grow; he delights to see us worship; and he delights to hear us pray. He is sitting on his throne at all times with his ear tuned to earth, delighting in the words, in the songs, and in the praises of God's people. God delights in us, and we delight in him.

Psalm 1 suggests the need for obedience, but it is an obedience that is generated by love and that springs from a transformed life. Obedience that is based upon legalism leads only to frustration. Obedience must flow out of our love for God. That is why Jesus said that the greatest commandment is that we love God wholeheartedly. If we love God with all our hearts, then it is not a burden to obey him and to do what he asks.

In light of the Scriptures mentioned above, 'delight' should be understood as a term of affection, and its prominence in Psalm 1 testifies to the importance of the passions in the life of the righteous. Psalm 1.2, however, is not alone in its affirmation that the righteous are those who take 'delight' in the Torah of Yahweh. A similar sentiment is echoed four times in Psalm 119 (vv. 70, 77, 92, and 174). Furthermore, the Psalter calls for not only a delight in the 'Torah' but also a delight in the Lord's 'statutes' (119.16), his 'testimonies' (119.24), and his 'commandments' (112.1; 119.47).

The delight of the believer in the Lord and in his Word is expressed in the following Scriptures:

> 'Delight yourself also in the LORD, And He shall give you the desires of your heart' (Ps. 37.4).

> 'I delight to do Your will, O my God, And Your law is within my heart' (Ps. 40.8).

> 'I will delight myself in Your statutes; I will not forget Your word' (Ps. 119.16).

The word 'delight' is not the only term that suggests the importance of affection for the Law. The writer of Psalm 119 declares, 'Oh, how I love your Law! It is my contemplation all the day' (v. 97, cf. vv. 113, 127, 140, 163, and 165). Psalm 19 praises God's 'law,' 'testimony,' 'precepts,' 'commandments,' and 'judgments,' saying, 'They are more desirable than gold, yes, than much fine gold: sweeter also than honey and the honeycomb' (v. 10, cf. Ps. 119.72, 103). Through the use of other affective terms the hearer of the Psalms is encouraged to put the Torah 'in his heart' (37.31; 40.8), to 'rejoice' in the Torah (119.14, 111, 162), to 'long for' God's precepts (119.40), to 'rejoice' in God's statutes (19.8), to 'desire' God's commandments

(119.131), to 'run' toward them (119.32), and to make them his 'songs' (119.54) and his 'desire'. The hearer is enjoined to 'rejoice' and 'be glad' because of God's judgments (48.11; 97.8). The psalmist pleads longingly, 'Open my eyes, that I may see wondrous things out of your Torah' (119.18, cf. v. 129). The tenor of the Psalms is similar to that of Jeremiah who exclaims, 'Your word was for me the joy and rejoicing of my heart' (Jer. 15.16).

The above Scriptures demonstrate a passionate disposition. To delight in the Torah is to rejoice in it, to love it, to long for it, to desire it more than gold, and to enjoy it more than honey. The words of the Torah penetrate the heart, stir the emotions, warn the intellect, and energize the will. The emphasis of Psalm 1 is not upon deeds but delight, not on duty but desire, not on obedience but on affections that are rightly oriented towards God. Psalm 1 points to the inner life of the heart that longs to hear God's voice and that welcomes God's Word with affection and joy. If we delight in the Word of God, we will read it, study it, search it, and allow it to speak into our lives.

The Righteous Meditate in the Word of God

But his delight is in the law of the LORD,
And in His law he meditates day and night (Ps. 1.2).

The righteous person delights in the Torah, and that delight is manifested through continual reflection upon it. The meaning of the Hebrew word *hagah*, translated here as 'meditate,' does not correspond exactly to the English 'meditate,' which means 'to exercise the mind in thought or reflection' (*Oxford English Dictionary*). While 'meditate' often denotes a silent activity, the Hebrew *hagah* seems in most cases to signify some sort of audible, vocal utterance. In the Hebrew dictionaries, it is defined as 'moan, growl, utter, speak, muse' (*BDB*, p. 211) and 'utter, mutter, moan, meditate, devise, plot' (*TWOT*, I, p. 468).

Observe how the word 'meditate' (*hagah*) is used in the following Scriptures:

'This book of the Torah shall not depart out of your mouth; you shall meditate in it day and night' (Josh. 1.8).

'My mouth will praise you with joyful lips. When I remember you on my bed, I meditate on you in the night watches' (Ps. 63.5b-6).

'I remember my song in the night … I will meditate on all your work, and muse on your mighty deeds' (Ps. 77.6-12).

'I remember the days of old; I meditate on all your works; I muse on the work of your hands' (Ps. 143.5).

In light of the fact that the Torah is to be in Joshua's 'mouth,' it seems likely that his meditation would include some form of utterance. Also, two of the above three examples from Psalms include parallels to the word 'muse' (Ps. 77.12 and 143.5), which may signify 'rehearsing' a matter and most often includes speech (Ps. 55.2, 18; 64.2; 69.13; 102.1; 105.2; 142.3). Furthermore, the context of singing is evident in Psalms 63 and 77; which suggests that in these texts meditation is expressed in a song of praise.

In the Hebrew, therefore, meditation likely denotes a thoughtful, deliberate utterance, which may be spoken or sung softly. Meditation on the Torah might be accomplished through the reading of the written text, as in the case of Josh. 1.8. Or for those who do not have access to the written Torah, meditation could be in the form of recitation from memory or of repeating the traditional narratives. Meditation might also signify the murmuring of one whose thoughts are occupied in deep reflection upon God's words and deeds. To meditate means to lose oneself in God's Word and to be filled with thoughts of God's deeds or his will. In Ps. 1.2, the word 'meditate' is an expression of innermost delight in the Word of God.

As shown in the Scriptures above, meditation can signify the utterance of a song; therefore, the meditation of Ps. 1.2 can include the singing of psalms as one of its modes of expression. Another connection between meditation and singing is the use of the word *higgaion*, which signifies a psalm of meditation (see Pss. 9.16 and 92.3). Still another connection between Torah and song, is that when Moses wrote the book of the Law, he also wrote a commemorative song (Deut. 31.22-24). The song is taught to the people, and the Book of the Law is handed over to the Levites and elders. Thus, Deuteronomy 31–32 identifies law-contemplation with worshipful song-singing. It is the song which will be forever known by the people (Deut. 31.21). Therefore, modes of biblical meditation include reading the Torah, reciting Scripture, and reflecting on the Word. Yet, the worshipful singing of psalms may be the form of meditation that is most appropriate to the context of Ps. 1.2.

Finally, it should not be overlooked that the commendation to meditate in the Torah appears within a psalm, suggesting perhaps that Psalm 1 itself becomes a demonstration of what is envisioned in 1.2. Therefore, as an introduction to the Psalter, Ps. 1.2 may conceive of the Psalms as passionate meditations on the Torah. Perhaps the singing of the Psalms is not the only way of taking delight in the Torah, but it is one way. It follows that the promise of 'blessedness' (Ps. 1.1) accrues to the person who reads, recites, and sings the Psalms with delight.

If we delight in the Word of God, we will spend much time absorbing its message. The psalmist declares that the righteous person delights in the Law of the Lord 'and in his law he meditates day and night' (Ps. 1.2). The believer should be continually occupied with thoughts of God and his Word. Meditation on the Law of the Lord requires a commitment of time. Modern readers often try to read through the Bible hurriedly, but this is a mistake. Reading the Bible is not improved by speed; there is no benefit to being in a hurry. In fact, you are a lot better off if you can find a place where you can read it out loud and slow down so that it can sink in as you think about it and meditate on it. You should read it and repeat it, because you are trying to get a firm grip on God's word.

The Righteous Flourish like a Fruitful Tree

He shall be like a tree planted by the rivers of water,
That brings forth its fruit in its season,
Whose leaf also shall not wither;
And whatever he does shall prosper (Ps. 1.3).

By meditating on God's Word, getting into it, reading it, going over it, and studying it, God will speak to you. Those who delight in the Law of the Lord and meditate in it will be like a flourishing tree. The person who does not do evil but delights in and meditates in God's word is like a tree planted by the rivers of water, bringing forth fruit in its season. His leaf does not wither, and whatsoever he does shall prosper. This is the blessedness of giving your heart and mind to God's word. If you remain in the Word of God, reading it, studying it, meditating on it, and obeying it, then God will surely direct your steps and you will be like a healthy, flourishing tree, nourished by the rivers of water.

The tree that is 'planted' by the rivers of waters is not a tree that springs up spontaneously, but one that is set out in a favorable place and that is cultivated with care. The word 'rivers' does not here quite express the sense of the original Hebrew. The Hebrew word *peleg* refers to irrigation channels, canals, trenches. The rivers of water are the irrigation channels, and the trees are planted there because it is a well-watered place. It is not an accidental thing; it is a planted tree. God plants us where we need to be, where we can prosper.

The righteous person is like a tree that brings forth fruit in season. The idea is that of a tree which, at the proper season of the year, is loaded with fruit. The image is one of great beauty and purpose. The fruit is not untimely. It does not ripen and fall too soon or fall before it is mature; and the crop is abundant.

Furthermore, his leaves do not wither. The leaves are unaffected by the heat of the sun and the drying effects of the hot winds. Like a tree that is green and flourishing, the person who delights in God's Word will be protected from every danger that comes their way.

Finally, 'whatsoever he does will prosper'. This tree is always healthy; it is extending its roots, circulating its sap, putting forth fruit-buds, blossoms, leaves, or fruit; all in their proper seasons. So the righteous person is ever extending deeper roots, growing stronger in grace, and increasing in the Holy Spirit. Much fruit to the glory and praise of God is continually produced.

If we desire to obtain permanent prosperity and happiness, it is to be found only by pursuing God and his Word. Jesus tells us, 'Seek first the kingdom of God and his righteousness and all these things will be added to you' (Mt. 6.33). Of course, we understand that we may sometimes face times of trouble and tribulation. Even the righteous are subject to the calamities that come upon a people in times of commercial distress, in seasons of war, famine, and pestilence. But still, a holy life will be followed by God's blessing, and the righteous will 'rejoice in the Lord always' (Phil. 4.4). It is this great and important truth which is the primary message of Psalm 1.

The Wicked Live Worthless Lives

The ungodly are not so,
  But are like the chaff which the wind drives away.
  (Ps. 1.4).

Unlike the righteous, the wicked person does not flourish and has no status among God's people. The wicked are not like a fruitful tree; instead, they are 'like the chaff which the wind drives away.' The wicked are like the chaff (also called 'husk') that is separated from the grain. The ancient process called 'winnowing' is in view here. After the farmers harvested the grain, they would beat it with a stick or have a cow trample it thoroughly. The beating and trampling would separate the grain from the husk. Then the farmer would throw the grain up in the air, and the wind would blow away the husk. If there was no wind at the time, the farmer would blow the husk away with a large fan. The husk that the wind blows away is worthless.

The wicked are not like a tree in any respect. They are not even like a decaying tree, a barren tree, a dead tree; for either of these would suggest some idea of stability or permanency. They may have their mansions, but those mansions will crumble. They may have their riches, but those riches will not endure. They may have their lands; but in the end, they will lose those lands because 'the meek shall inherit the earth' (Ps. 37.11). They are like dry and worthless chaff driven off by the wind. They are of no value at all; they are intrinsically worthlessness. They are worthless to both God and to their fellow humans. In spite of their boasting, their riches, and their high positions, they are worthless in regard to all the purposes for which God made them.

The idea of the wicked being like chaff is picked up in the Gospel of Matthew, where John the Baptist proclaims, 'His winnowing fan is in His hand, and He will thoroughly clean out His threshing floor, and gather His wheat into the barn; but He will burn up the chaff with unquenchable fire' (Mt. 3.12). John's prophecy leads us to consider the next verse of Psalm 1.

The Wicked Are Without Standing

**Therefore the ungodly shall not stand in the judgment,
Nor sinners in the congregation of the righteous
(Ps. 1.5).**

In verse 5, we learn first that the wicked have no standing in the judgment. The idea seems to be derived from the act of standing up to be tried, or to receive a sentence. However, when they come to be judged, they will have nothing to plead on their behalf. Therefore, they will be condemned, and they will be unable to remain standing. Their knees will buckle from terror and dread of the sentence of guilt. In Rev. 6.17, John speaks of the days of great tribulation; and he says, 'For the great day of His wrath has come, and who is able to stand?'

We also learn in Ps.1.5 that the sinners have no place in the congregation of the righteous. The sinners are not reckoned or regarded as belonging to the righteous. In all the places where the righteous are assembled, the sinners will have no place. Where God's people assemble to worship God, the sinners have no place. Where the righteous stand in God's presence to glorify his holy name, the sinners have no place. Where the righteous gather in heaven and are gathered together to receive their reward, the sinner has no place. The sinner has no place in the congregation of the people of God.

The righteous long for heaven, for no evil will dwell there. On earth, the church is impure – the tares grow in the same field as the wheat (Mt. 13.25-40). Like Lot, whose righteous soul was tormented by the sinful deeds of the people of Sodom (2 Pet. 2.8), we are continually distressed by the sinfulness of our generation. But there will be no sin in heaven. We are told in Rev. 21.8, 'But the cowardly, unbelieving, abominable, murderers, sexually immoral, sorcerers, idolaters, and all liars shall have their part in the lake which burns with fire and brimstone, which is the second death.' Sinners have no place in the assembly of the righteous.

Having no place, it follows that they have no authority or power there. The tyrants of the world are powerless and helpless in the assembly of the saints. Abusers of the weak will face judgment at the hands of the Almighty avenger, who is the father of the orphan and husband to the widow. Even now there exist two worlds, the kingdom of this world and the kingdom of God. In large part, the sinners rule this world; but in the kingdom of God, sinners have no influence. The church stands as a beacon of light in this darkness and as a refuge for those who have suffered at the hands of Satan and his servants.

The Wicked are Destroyed in the End

**For the LORD knows the way of the righteous,
But the way of the ungodly shall perish (Ps. 1.6).**

There is a reason that the righteous are like a flourishing tree. There is a reason that the wicked are like worthless chaff and that they cannot stand in the judgment. All of these truths are based upon one foundation – 'the Lord knows'. In the book of Exodus, the Israelites were slaves in Egypt and they were struggling and made to serve the Egyptians. They cried out to God because of their taskmasters and because of the hard bondage. But the Lord heard their groaning and their sighs because of their taskmasters. We read that 'the Lord knew' (Exod. 2.25). The psalmist declares that the Lord knows the way of the righteous, whether it is good or whether it is bad. The Lord knows, he sees, and he hears. Though we walk through the valley of the shadow of death, the Lord knows our way and guides us with his staff. He numbers the hairs of our heads, and he will not allow us to fall. Job said, 'He knows the way that I take; when he has tried me, I shall come forth as gold' (Job 23.10).

The Lord knows our pathway, but the way of the wicked is for destruction. 'Perish' means to be destroyed, to be wiped out. Their destruction may not be immediate; but it is sure, as we learn later on in Psalm 73. There, for example, the psalmist complains that the wicked are prospering. However, he writes, 'But then I went to the house of God and I learned of their end.' Their end is destruction. Their projects, designs, and operations will perish; and in the day of judgment, they shall be condemned to the everlasting lake of fire. 'As wax melts before fire, so the wicked shall perish before the presence of God' (Ps. 68.2).

Conclusion

Many significant lessons can be learned from the study of Psalm 1. Let us review what we have studied and reflect on the implications of this Psalm.

Psalm 1 Emphasizes the Value of Teaching

The first Psalm contains no prayer, and it contains no praise. It is a teaching psalm, a psalm of instruction. Psalms of instruction are songs that help us to draw closer to God through their guidance. Some people call these the wisdom psalms, because many of the topics in these psalms are also found in the wisdom books of Proverbs, Ecclesiastes, and Job. These characteristic themes are the family, God's law, justice, life's choices, life's inconsistencies, the trust or fear of God, and the contrast between the wicked person and the righteous person. The following chart shows the presence of these themes in Psalms 1, 73, and 128.

	Ps. 1	Ps. 73	Ps. 128
The wicked and the righteous	1-3, 4-6		
God's retribution	3, 6	18, 19, 27	2, 5
God's law	2		
Trust/fear of God		21-24	1, 4
Inconsistencies of life		1-20	
Family			3, 6

Other Psalms of Instruction are Psalms 32, 37, 49, 78, 112, 119, 127, 133, and 145.

The presence of these wisdom psalms within Israel's song book suggests the importance of instruction as a part of worship. The biblical example of worship includes the discipleship component. The book of Psalms begins with teaching and includes teaching throughout the book. We will learn in other psalms that prayer and praise are valuable aspects of worship; but the very first psalm emphasizes worship as a learning experience, and the curriculum for learning is the 'law of the LORD' (Ps. 1.2). We read in the New Testament that when the early Christians gathered together for worship, they combined teaching, fellowship, eating, praying, and praise:

they continued steadfastly in the teaching of the apostles and in fellowship, in the breaking of bread, and in prayers … with one accord in the temple, and breaking bread from house to house … praising God (Acts 2.42-47).

Psalm 1 Invites Us to Hear God's Word

Psalm 1 pronounces the Lord's approval of and blessings upon those who are righteous. The righteous are identified by their resistance to the lure of wicked counsel and by their affection for the 'law of the LORD.' The psalm points to the passions rather than to behavior as the key element of the righteous person – 'his delight is in the Torah of the LORD and in his Torah he meditates day and night' (Ps. 1.2). Instead of demanding legalistic obedience to the Law, Psalm 1 evokes a passion for the Law. The blessed ones are thus identified by the attitude of their hearts – their love for God's Word. Psalm 1.2 teaches us that delight in the Torah is the determining and effective disposition of the truly happy life.

In its role as an introduction to the Psalter, Psalm 1 sets the tone for encountering the Psalms, identifying the attitude that is necessary to enter the Psalter. Psalm 1 suggests that right worship begins with rightly oriented affections. When Psalm 1 invites meditation on the Torah as a response to God's self-revelation, it becomes its own passionate example. It offers itself as a model of Torah meditation, a model which is picked up and expanded by the psalms that follow. The Psalms, therefore, serve as exemplars of what it means to delight in the Torah of the Lord.

Psalm 1 Guarantees Happiness to the Righteous

Our lives are filled with uncertainties, and our children are faced with competing viewpoints of how they should live their lives. They see the lifestyles of the wealthy and the behavior of sports heroes and movie stars, and they question the value of serving God in this world. Is there really joy in living for Jesus, or can we find an equal amount of joy in serving ourselves? Are the poor in spirit really blessed, or is it the proud and arrogant who find prosperity? Are those who hunger and thirst for righteousness really filled, or should they instead settle for the 'lust of the flesh, the lust of the eyes, and the pride of life' (1 Jn 2.16)? Does the universe operate according to dependable laws in which good is rewarded and evil is punished? Does God really care? If so, is he involved in the outcomes of our decisions?

Psalm 1 assures us that God honors our faithfulness, that evil will be punished and good will be rewarded. In spite of the apparent randomness in the universe, Psalm 1 guarantees that God's Law governs the destiny of us all. God cares for his people, and God acts on their behalf. Yes, there is joy in serving the Lord – 'joy unspeakable and full of glory' (1 Pet. 1.8). Yes, God knows who we are and where we live. It is God's providence that guarantees the blessedness of the righteous and the destruction of the wicked.

Connecting with the Psalm

(Questions for discussion)

In what ways are you 'blessed'?

Can you think of examples that would illustrate Ps. 1.1?

What can the church do to strengthen our love for God's Word?

How would you define 'prosperity'?

How does Psalm 1 encourage you and give you hope?

What if ... ?

(Creative and imaginative ideas)

What if we prayerfully examine our lives in light of Ps. 1.1 and list areas where we are tempted?

What if we schedule a time and a place for studying God's Word and make that appointment a priority?

What if we take time to give thanks for God's provision in our lives?

Now, come up with your own 'What if ... ?'

2

THE PASSIONATE PURSUIT OF EFFECTIVE PRAYER: PSALM 13

Setting the Direction

I was awakened early one morning by the ringing of the telephone. As a pastor, I knew that a phone call that early in the morning usually indicated either an emergency or a tragedy. The caller confirmed that a tragedy indeed had occurred. My former college roommate, now a pastor, had committed suicide. This news came as a terrible shock, and I was filled with disbelief. In college, my roommate had been a spiritual example to me. His level of devotion to God, the depth of his prayers, the genuineness of his faith, his willingness to sacrifice and bear the cross, his passion to win the lost, and his exuberant generosity were evident to all who knew him. Having been his close friend, I found it difficult to comprehend how he could have lost hope to the extent that he would take his own life.

I learned later that my friend had gotten caught up in the prosperity gospel. He had come to believe that those who are righteous will always be blessed with spiritual and material prosperity. He had come to believe that the righteous are always victorious and that by faith they will quickly defeat all opposition that comes their way. His overwhelming disappointment and unscriptural expectation of prosperity had paralyzed his hope, and he had not achieved a worry-free life. According to the prosperity gospel, believers will live in perfect health – sickness is a result of unbelief. My friend, however, was disappointed in his inability to reach the level of faith that he believed was required to live in perfect health and in continual victory. Consequently, he was unable to come to grips with the inconsistencies that developed between his idea of prosperity and the realities that he faced. My friend could not bear the thought that his faith was insufficient. His despair grew so intense that it drove him to suicide.

What my friend needed to know was that the prosperity gospel is insufficient – it is an incomplete gospel. It focuses upon only one side of the biblical picture of faith. He also needed to understand that his struggles were nothing new – the ancient Israelites faced similar theological tensions. We learned in Psalm 1 that the righteous are blessed, and the wicked are punished. The Lord knows the way of the righteous, and he insures that they are prosperous. Psalm 1 presents a world that operates according to divinely established rules and principles. It suggests a theology in which justice prevails in the world – the righteous are blessed and the wicked are punished.

The worldview of Psalm 1 is affirmed in Psalm 2 where the blessings of righteousness are extended to rulers and to nations. We learn that the 'nations rage … against the Lord and against his anointed' (Ps. 2.1-2), and these rebellious nations are broken and destroyed by the power of God (v. 9). In contrast, nations who 'serve the Lord with fear' can rejoice, because 'Blessed are all those who put their trust in him' (vv. 11-12).

However, if we stop reading after Psalm 2, our theology will be incomplete. Psalm 3 presents another side of the biblical picture of faith in which the neat, tidy, well-ordered theology of Psalms 1 and 2 gives way to a theology that allows for the realities of life – realities that include struggle, injustice, abuse, doubt, fear, and the testing of our faith.

Immediately after we hear in Psalms 1 and 2 that God blesses the righteous, we run up against these words in Psalm 3:

> ^{1} Oh Lord, those who trouble me are increased.
>   Many are they who rise up against me.
> ^{2} Many are saying to me,
>   'There is no help for you in God'.

In Psalm 3, the psalmist is challenged and tested, and his faith is put on trial. Likewise, in Ps. 13.1-2, we hear David pray,

¹ How long, O Lord? Will You forget me forever?
   How long will You hide Your face from me?
² How long shall I take counsel in my soul,
   Having sorrow in my heart daily?
   How long will my enemy be exalted over me?

Psalms 3 and 13 teach us that the righteous will face suffering, trials, and tests. These prayer psalms reflect the experience of righteous Job. The Bible declares that Job was 'perfect and upright; he feared God and shunned evil' (Job 1.1). Satan appeared before God and accused Job of being a 'fair weather' believer. Satan said to God, 'You put a hedge of protection around him. If you take away the hedge, Job will curse you to your face'. God had confidence in Job's faith and replied to Satan, 'I will remove my protection over Job and you may attack him in whatever way you like, only do not take his life'. Consequently, Job's faith was tested. Job, however, did not understand what was happening to him; he did not know what was going on. All he knew was that his children had been killed; his property had been destroyed and his houses knocked down; his cattle and his sheep had been stolen, his body was sick from head to toe, and he was sitting on an ash heap, asking God to just let him die because he was in misery.

The theology of Psalms 1 and 2 is important as a foundation to our relationship with God. It is vital that we are able to trust in God's goodness, sovereignty, and providence. We must also understand, however, that our faith in God will be tested – yes, our faith *must* be tested. The righteousness of Job resulted in prosperity, but then Job's faith was tested through suffering. Job's suffering did not come to him because of his weakness or failure but because of his strength of character and his trust in the Lord. Jesus promises, 'In the world you shall have tribulation' (Jn 16.33), and Paul declares, 'Those who live godly in Christ Jesus will suffer persecution' (2 Tim. 3.12). To those who suffer, Peter writes, 'Beloved, do not think it strange concerning the fiery trial which is to try you, as though some strange thing happened to you' (1 Pet. 4.12). Testings, trials, hardships, and sufferings are not a sign that we have failed; rather, they are a normal part of the Christian life, and their purpose is to make us stronger.

Some would say that we ought to live in Psalm 1; and when suffering comes our way, we need only to speak a positive confession and ignore our problem. Psalm 3, Psalm 13, and other Scriptures, however, would tell us that life is not so simple. There are days when our rejoicing turns to mourning and God's blessing upon our life is in doubt. Our lives are turned upside down because tragedy, trouble, upheaval, chaos, confusion, and uncertainty come our way. We do not know why it comes or how it happens. When Jesus' disciples heard that Pilate had killed a number of Galilean Jews and mixed their blood with the sacrifices, they questioned Jesus as to how this sort of thing could happen to God's people. Jesus explained to his disciples that righteous people sometimes suffer.

> And Jesus answered and said to them, 'Do you suppose that these Galileans were worse sinners than all other Galileans, because they suffered such things? I tell you, no … Or those eighteen on whom the tower in Siloam fell and killed them, do you think that they were worse sinners than all other men who dwelt in Jerusalem? I tell you, no …' (Lk. 13.2-5).

Jesus did not offer a reason why the Galilean Jews were made to suffer, and he did not explain why the tower fell on the people of Siloam. But he did insist that their suffering was not on account of their sin or disobedience. Jesus taught us that suffering is a part of living in this world. Until the kingdom of God is fully realized, Christians will face tests and trials.

In this chapter, we will study Psalm 13, and we will learn how to respond to experiences of pain and testing. When we are really hurting, we need to be able to take our hurts to God in passionate prayer.

Discussion Starters

Discuss the value of prayer in your own life.

Share a time when God answered an urgent prayer.

In light of 1 Pet. 1.6-7 and Jas 1.2-4, how would you explain the goals and purposes of testing and suffering?

Hearing the Word of God

Psalm 13

To the Chief Musician. A Psalm of David.

[1] How long, O LORD? Will You forget me forever?
How long will You hide Your face from me?
[2] How long shall I take counsel in my soul,
Having sorrow in my heart daily?
How long will my enemy be exalted over me?
[3] Consider and hear me, O LORD my God;
Enlighten my eyes, Lest I sleep the sleep of death;
[4] Lest my enemy say, 'I have prevailed against him';
Lest those who trouble me rejoice when I am moved.
[5] But I have trusted in Your mercy;
My heart shall rejoice in Your salvation.
[6] I will sing to the LORD,
Because He has dealt bountifully with me.

Introduction: The Psalms of Prayer

The psalms of prayer are passionate pleas born out of pain. They are urgent prayers that may be motivated by several categories of need. They may be prayers for overcoming the enemy, prayers for healing, or prayers of repentance because of sin. For example, in Psalm 51 David prays, 'Wash me thoroughly from my iniquity, and cleanse me from my sin' (v. 2). These different kinds of prayers have a similar form that Bible scholars call the 'lament' or 'lamentation'. The lament (what I have called the psalm of prayer) is the most common type of Psalm in the Bible. You probably have observed that one entire book of the Bible is made up of lament and carries the name 'Lamentations'.

Psalm 13 is a lament – an urgent, passionate prayer. It follows a short, simple, and straightforward pattern that stands as an example of how these prayers are expressed in the Psalms. Psalm 13 teaches us how to bring our needs to God in prayer. If we take David's prayer in Psalm 13 as our example, we find six pointers to effective prayer.

First, David Speaks Directly to God.

The psalmist cries out to God saying,

> **How long, O LORD? Will You forget me forever?**
> **How long will You hide Your face from me? (Ps. 13.1)**

Although we know that everything *works* for good to them that love God (Rom. 8.28), not everything *feels* good. We are never told in the Bible to ignore these bad things; we are told to take them to God in prayer. In addition to the Psalms, Phil. 4.6 says,

> But in everything with prayer and thanksgiving let your requests be made known unto God; and the peace of God that passes all understanding will keep your heart and mind through Christ Jesus.

Paul exhorts us to take everything – every need, every trial, every burden – to God in prayer.

Psalm 13 begins like many other psalms of prayer by speaking directly to God. Unlike some psalms that speak only *about* God, the laments speak *to* God. It is one thing to talk about God, but it is another thing to talk to God. David says directly to God, 'How long, oh Lord, will you forget me? Forever?' (v. 1). So the prayers in the book of Psalms start out speaking directly to God. Sometimes it is helpful to share our burdens with our pastor, our family, and other believers; but sharing with other people cannot take the place of prayer. There is no valid substitute for fervent prayer. Other laments also begin with the psalmist addressing God pointedly.

'Unto thee will I cry, O LORD my rock' (Ps. 28.1).

'Hear my cry, O God, listen to my prayer' (Ps. 61.1).

'Hear my voice, O God, in my complaint; preserve my life from dread of the enemy' (Ps. 64.1).

'Save me, O God; for the waters are come in unto my soul' (Ps. 69.1).

'Deliver me, O LORD' (Ps. 140.1).

'Lord, I cry unto thee: make haste unto me' (Ps. 141.1).

'Hear my prayer, O LORD' (Ps. 143.1).

'Out of the depths I cry to thee, O LORD!' (Ps. 130.1).

Second, David Expresses the Pain of Abandonment.

> **How long, O LORD? Will You forget me forever?**
> **How long will You hide Your face from me? (Ps. 13.1)**

The psalmist feels abandoned, and he pleads with God: 'Will You forget me forever?' This second part of the lament makes plain the feeling of not knowing, the feeling of uncertainty. If we do not feel sure about our trials, it is all right to tell God about our doubts because he already knows what is in our hearts.

David feels like God has forgotten about him, even though he knows he has not. He is asking, 'Lord, have you forgotten me? Will you forget me forever? How long will this go on?' This is how he is feeling in the presence of the Lord, and he brings an honest statement before him: 'How long will you hide your face from me?' You may never have felt like God was hidden from you; or maybe you have been hiding from God, like Adam did. Most of us, at some point, have gone through a dark valley where we felt like we could not find God and like our prayers were just bouncing off the ceiling.

Denial of our pain is not an option. Attempting to ignore our problems will not make them go away. The lament psalms encourage us to engage in faithful and legitimate protest to God. When we are in trouble, we should pour out our souls to him in prayer.

Third, David States His Problem.

The third characteristic of the lament psalm is found in verse two:

> **How long will I take counsel in my soul,**
> **having sorrow in my heart;**
> **and how long will my enemy be exalted over me? (Ps. 13.2)**

David names his problem; he voices his complaint. He is sorrowful because the enemy has gotten the advantage over him. The enemy, however, is not named specifically. When we read, 'My enemy is exalted over me', we do not know the identity of the enemy or how the enemy is attacking David. All we know is that David is in sorrow and that he is suffering because of the attacks of the enemy. The psalm is specific enough that we can name the problem, but it is vague enough that we are able to place ourselves in David's place. Thus, we can pray David's prayer and make it our own.

It is common in the Psalms for people to cry out to God and to voice their complaint. For example, in Psalm 55 the psalmist says, 'My heart is in anguish within me, and the terror of death has fallen upon me'; and in Ps. 64.1 he pleads, 'preserve me from the dread of the enemy'. In Psalm 69 he prays, 'Save me, oh God; the waters have come up unto my soul'. In Psalm 120 he says, 'In my distress I cried to the Lord'; and in Psalm 142 he says, 'I pour out my complaint before God'. In Psalm 107 the people cry unto the Lord in their trouble; and Psalm 130 says, 'Out of the depths I cried unto the Lord'. Outside the book of Psalms Jonah says in Jonah 2.2, 'Out of the belly of hell I cried unto you, oh Lord'.

In the New Testament, Paul talks about God comforting us in our trouble. He writes, 'The sufferings of Christ are in us' (2 Cor. 1.5), we are afflicted, and we endure suffering. He then states, 'We were burdened beyond measure, above strength, so that we despaired even of life itself' (2 Cor. 1.8). Paul was so burdened that he thought he was going to die; and he says, 'We had the sentence of death, but God delivered us'. In 2 Corinthians 12, Paul had a thorn in the flesh, and he explains, 'I prayed to the Lord three times that it might be removed'; but God said, 'My grace is sufficient for you, for my strength is made perfect in weakness'. Through this Paul learns, 'So I will glory in my affliction'; and he brings that burden unto the Lord.

Sorrow and grief are things that are common throughout the Bible. In Mt. 5.4, Jesus teaches, 'Blessed are they that mourn, for they shall be comforted'. In James 4, the apostle says, 'Lament and mourn and weep; let your laughter be turned to mourning and your joy into gloom, and humble yourselves in the sight of the Lord'; and James says further, 'Is anyone among you suffering? Let him pray' (Jas 5.13). Similarly, the Apostle Paul says, 'Rejoice with those that rejoice and weep with those that weep' (Rom. 12.15). Finally, in his vision of heaven, John sees the souls of those that had died under the altar; and they ask, 'How long, oh Lord, how long until you judge and avenge our blood on those that dwell on the earth?' (Rev. 6.10)

The psalms of lament give voice to our suffering and to our pain. The laments teach us that we should come openly and honestly to God with our needs; we should tell him our doubts and our fears. In doing so, we can be assured that God will not reject us. Jesus declared that God's house should be a house of prayer, but many churches no longer include altar calls, prayer for the sick, and times of seeking the face of God. We have turned worship into entertainment, and we have changed the preaching of the Gospel into self-help sessions and positive thinking philosophy. There is little time given to minister to those who are suffering.

There must be a place among God's people where we can weep with those that weep. When we come to church, some people are ready to rejoice and praise the Lord; but other people are in the bottom of the pit, and they need someone to pray with them. They need to be able to come down to the altar to weep and to cry and to get help by calling on God. Somehow, we must make room for earnest prayer in our church. It would not be appropriate for us to make every church service like a funeral, but neither is it right for us to ignore the needs of those who are suffering.

Many of our brothers and sisters come to church after having received a disconcerting report from the doctor. The people of the church should gather around these and pray for them. Others arrive at church bearing a heavy burden of grief. During times of prayer at the altar, the body of Christ can respond to their pain, so that grieving ones are not alone in that moment. As they mourn and grieve, we as brothers and sisters should join with them, mourn with them, and weep with them.

Fourth, David Pleads for God's Intervention.
David has expressed the pain that he is suffering, and he has stated his complaint. Now he pleads with God to come to his aid. He says to God,

> ³ **Consider and hear me, O LORD my God;**
>   **Enlighten my eyes, Lest I sleep the sleep of death;**
> ⁴ **Lest my enemy say, 'I have prevailed against him';**
>   **Lest those who trouble me rejoice when I am moved**
>   **(Ps. 13.3-4).**

David brings his specific need to God and says, 'God, I need your help'. He is not whining, grumbling, or murmuring. God does not honor the grumblings of complainers. Look at the example of the Israelites in the wilderness when God rained down manna from heaven; and they started grumbling and complaining, 'We're getting tired of this manna'. David's prayer is different from the complaining of the Israelites – he has a legitimate need. He is suffering real pain, and he appeals to God by saying, 'O God, hear my prayer. Consider me and hear me'.

Fifth, David Trusts God.

David's urgent and passionate prayer is based on a relationship of trust. He says to God,

> **But I have trusted in your mercy;**
> **My heart shall rejoice in your salvation (Ps. 13.5).**

Even though David does not know why he is suffering, he knows that somehow God is in control of things.

The psalmist's confession of trust in God signals a transition from lament to praise. Notice that in verse five, David's prayer turns in a different direction. He had come to God; he had talked about his feelings of being abandoned; he had laid out his complaint and his suffering; and he had prayed a specific prayer. But now he says, 'I have trusted in your mercy'. This is a declaration of faith and trust in God. David has offered up his complaint and he has faithfully brought his need before God. God hears the kind of prayer that says, 'I have trusted in your mercy'.

The word 'mercy' is a covenant word that suggests a relationship of mutual loyalty. David can trust God, because they are walking to-gether in covenant. Time and time again David has experienced God's faithfulness. Just as God delivered David from the mouth of the lion and from the attack of Goliath, so he will deliver him from this threat as well.

The second part of verse 5 says, 'My heart *shall* rejoice in your salvation'. In other words, David is confident that God will do some-thing. Perhaps David has 'prayed through' to victory. Now, in the midst of trouble, he is *not* in a rejoicing mood; but soon he will rejoice again. Today may be Friday, but Sunday is coming. We will not be down all of the time. David can say, 'Yea, though I walk through the valley of the shadow of death, I will fear no evil' (Ps. 23.4). I may be walking through the valley now, but I will come out of the valley. I will *not* stay in the valley forever. I *will* rejoice! We must pray with full confidence and deep trust in God and his faithfulness.

Sixth and Finally, David Promises to Praise God.
These Psalms of urgent prayer, these laments, are uttered by people who are suffering but who also are fully committed to praise. The lament does not last forever: 'Weeping may endure for a night, but joy comes in the morning' (Ps. 30.5). In the last verse, the psalmist says,

> **I will sing to the LORD,**
> **Because He has dealt bountifully with me (Ps. 13.6).**

Here, David makes a commitment to 'sing unto the Lord'. Some of these lament psalms go even further than a promise to sing. They make a promise to bring an offering to the temple, saying something like this: 'when the answer comes, I will offer up a sacrifice of praise'. That is, 'I will go down to the house of God and offer up a thanksgiving sacrifice'. In biblical times, the Jews had what they called a thanksgiving offering, and many of these prayer psalms include a 'vow of praise'. The vow of praise means that when the prayer is answered, the person will go to the temple and will offer up a sacrifice of praise unto God.

These prayer psalms have a kind of progression in them. They start out with a raw expression of pain, such as 'O, Lord, how long' or 'where are you' or 'I cannot even see you and I cannot feel you' or 'Lord, help me'. The psalmist then moves to an expression of faith, saying, 'I know you will help me, I know you will hear me, and I will praise you!'. They begin in describing the trouble, and they end in confessing God's greatness and God's goodness. Should we pray the same kind of prayers today? Jesus did so – right there on the cross he prayed, 'My God, my God, why have you forsaken me?' He prays the prayer from Psalm 22. The Lord Jesus himself prayed this kind of prayer, feeling that forsakenness and feeling like God was far away and that he was nowhere to be found. Yet sometimes we do not know whether we should give voice to our pain or ignore our pain and just praise God for his promises.

On May 17, 2008, I was awakened by a severe pain in the center of my chest. I took two aspirin and soon the pain turned into a feeling of pressure, like someone sitting on my chest. I sat down at my desk, and I tried to pray. However, I could not think of any words to say, so I leaned back in my chair, closed my eyes, and said, 'Jesus, Jesus, Jesus'. When we cannot say anything else, we can call on Jesus, and he knows what is in our hearts. As I called out his name, I began to realize and to know that I was in touch with Jesus. My heart might be causing me some problems, but Jesus was still on the throne. After a time of prayer and seeking God, he gave me a sense of great peace. I was reminded of David's words, 'I shall not die but live and declare the works of the Lord' (Ps. 118.17). I was able to put my trust in Jesus and say, 'My heart shall rejoice in your salvation; I will sing unto the Lord'. Later in the day, when the symptoms continued, I entered the hospital and eventually had heart surgery. Today, I am completely recovered.

If we will take things to God in prayer and not try to hide our pain, amazing things will happen. We should never pretend that we need no help. We *do* need help. We need Jesus. We need to call on him, to call on his name. Some people want to shout and to rejoice, but they do not want to pray. Shouting and rejoicing is an important part of worship; but if we have not really touched Jesus, then we have nothing to shout about. If we have not touched Jesus, if we have not given him our burdens, then once we cease our shouting and go home, the burdens will still be laying heavy upon us. We must give our burdens to Jesus, and then we can shout with liberty in our soul. This kind of urgent prayer has been given a name; we call it 'praying through'. This is calling upon God until we have touched God and we know that he has heard our prayer. It is not just *saying* a prayer, rather, it is praying until that confidence and assurance and trust comes down from heaven. It is praying until we feel like God is saying, 'I have heard your prayer and I will act on your behalf'. We may not know exactly *what* he will do, but we know that he will do *something*. He may say, 'Yes'; he may say, 'No'; or he may say, 'Wait'; but we are content to rest in God's hands.

Conclusion

The Suffering of the Righteous
We learn in Psalms 1 and 2 that the righteous are blessed and the wicked are punished. The foundation of our faith is that God rules the world according to divinely established rules and principles. Psalm 13, however, presents the other side of the biblical picture of

faith, which allows for the realities of life, realities that include struggle, injustice, abuse, doubt, fear, and the testing of our faith.

Psalm 13 teaches us that the righteous will face suffering, trials, and tests. These prayer psalms reflect the experience of Abraham (Gen. 22.1), Joseph (Genesis 37), David, Job, Jeremiah, the Apostles, and even Jesus himself. In times of pain, Psalm 13 will show us a pattern for praying our way to victory.

Prayer Psalms Simplified
We have learned that the most common type of psalm is the Prayer Psalm, which Bible scholars call 'the lament'. The lament is the worshiper's passionate cry to God for deliverance from distress. The sufferer's trouble may take the form of sickness (Psalm 6), personal or corporate sin (Psalm 51), oppression (Psalm 10), or an accusation (Psalm 17). The lament usually begins with an address to God, followed by the specific complaint or need. The worshiper confesses trust in God and offers up a petition to God. The lament may include a declaration of assurance that God has heard the prayer and then conclude with a promise to praise God with a thanksgiving offering. Note the following example of the lament (Psalm 54).

1. Address to God
   'O God, save me' (v. 1)
2. Complaint (reason for the prayer)
   'strangers have risen up against me
   and oppressors have sought after my life' (v. 3)
3. Confession of trust in God
   'Behold, God is my helper' (v. 4)
4. Petition for help
   'Vindicate me … Hear my prayer' (vv. 1-2)
5. Assurance of being heard
   'He has delivered me out of all trouble' (v. 7)
6. Vow of praise offering
   'I will freely sacrifice unto You; I will praise Your
   name, O LORD' (v. 6).

The Prayer Psalms teach us the importance of being open and honest with God. In our religious circles, we often mask our true feelings. When it comes to our relationship with God, the psalms teach us that we can be totally open and honest with God.

Furthermore, the psalms of lament teach us that we should make a place for prayer in our worship services. Many churches have turned worship into nothing but celebration, and they have relegated prayer to the back rooms. Biblical worship provides a time and place for passionate prayer, for crying out to God. The New Testament instructs us to include times of prayer for people in the congregation (Jas 5.13-18). We are to 'be anxious for nothing, but in everything by prayer and supplication, let [our] requests be made known unto God' (Phil. 4.6). Peter says, 'casting all your care upon him, because he cares for you' (1 Pet. 5.7). The early church prayed together in times of need (Acts 1.14; 2.42; 3.1; 4.31; 6.4, 6; 8.15; 12.5; 13.1-3; 14.23; 16.13, 25; 20.36).

The lament psalms include Psalms 3-7, 9-14, 16, 17, 22, 25-28, 31, 35, 36, 38-40, 42-44, 51-64, 69-71, 74, 77, 79, 80, 83, 85, 86, 88, 90, 94, 102, 106, 108, 109, 120, 123, 126, 130, 137, and 140-143.

We must include prayer as an important part of our worship services. When we come together for worship, not everything we do is praise. We also give testimony to one another; we tell each other what we have been doing; we visit and we encourage one another,;we teach, we preach, and we pray. Prayer is a vital component of genuine worship. On any given Sunday, a large portion of any congregation will consist of people who are hurting severely. The most meaningful and helpful thing we can do for them in the service is to reach out to them. They need more than a sermon. They need more than uplifting songs. They need the touch of caring brothers and sisters in Christ. They need a church that will spend time with them in prayer until the Holy Spirit breaks through to victory.

Psalm 13 Personalized

If we find it difficult to say the right words and to speak forth our pain, we might want to use the following exercise as a way of starting the process of urgent prayer. We can write our name where David's name stands. We can write our need where David's need is listed. We can list our trouble, our feelings, and our specific request. We can take this version of Psalm 13, our own personal version, and come before God saying, 'Here is my need Lord. I am giving my pain to you. Please help me'.

A Psalm of _____.
           (your name)

¹ How long, O LORD? Will You forget me forever?
   How long will You hide Your face from me?
² How long _____
              (tell your trouble)
   Having _____ in my heart daily?
          (express your painful feeling)
   How long will _____?
                   (restate your suffering)
³ Consider and hear me, O LORD my God;

_____

                (state your prayer to God)
⁴ Lest my enemy say, 'I have prevailed against them';
   Lest those who trouble me rejoice when I am moved.
⁵ But I have trusted in Your mercy;
   My heart shall rejoice in Your salvation.
⁶ I will sing to the LORD,
   Because He has dealt bountifully with me.

Whenever we have a burden in our heart, but we cannot put together the right words, we should open up the book of Psalms and read through the prayers. In the Psalms we will find a prayer that will express our pain. We can make the psalm our own personal prayer, and God will honor it. The Psalms are God's word; they are prayers of David and of other saints of God. We can make them *our* prayers. Then, in addition to this help from the psalmist, we must submit ourselves to the Holy Spirit, who will pray through us 'with groanings that cannot be uttered' (Rom. 8.26). We must pursue effective prayer.

Connecting with the Psalm

(Questions for discussion)

> We know that God never leaves us, but have you ever felt like God was distant or felt like God had abandoned you?
>
> If you have ever suffered chronic pain or depression, you may want to share your experience with your group.
>
> Have you experienced what we call 'praying through'?
>
> What is the basis of our faith when we pray? Why do we trust God to answer?
>
> What is the value of knowing God as our 'Heavenly Father'?

What if … ?

(Creative and imaginative ideas)

> What if we prayerfully identify and list areas where we are struggling and then cry out to God about those areas?
>
> What if we make a list of reasons why we should pray?
>
> What if we share with the group why we trust God to answer?
>
> What if we create and/or join a prayer group?
>
> Now, come up with your own 'What if … ?'

3

THE PASSIONATE PURSUIT OF GOD'S PRESENCE: PSALM 22

Setting the Direction

Psalm 22 might be called 'Pain, Praises, and the Passion of Christ'. The Psalm is quoted in the New Testament in relation to the crucifixion of Jesus. At Calvary, Jesus endured great pain as he suffered for the sins of the world. As he hung upon the cross, suspended as a mediator between heaven and earth, he cried out to his heavenly father, 'My God, my God, why have you forsaken me?' (Mt. 27.46; Mk 15.34). Jesus took the words of his ancestor David and appropriated them to his own hour of pain. These words cited by Jesus, words of the ancient psalmist, cause us to ask the question, 'Where is God's presence when we are suffering?'

Songs of Prophecy

The writers of the New Testament found in the Psalms many testimonies to Jesus Christ. Christians have viewed the Psalms as predictive of the birth, life, death, and teachings of Jesus. Jesus himself quoted from the Psalms many times; and in the entire New Testament we find over one hundred quotations from the Psalms. Portions of the Psalms that are commonly cited as Messianic include the following:

Ps. 2.1-2	Opposition to the Messiah
Ps. 2.7	The divinity of Jesus
Ps. 2.9	The rule of Jesus

Ps. 16.8-11   The resurrection of Jesus
Ps. 22   The crucifixion of Jesus
Ps. 31.5   The death of Jesus
Ps. 34.20   Jesus' bones not broken
Ps. 40.6-8   The faithfulness of Jesus
Ps. 41.9   Messiah betrayed by a friend
Ps. 69.4   The rejection of Jesus
Ps. 69.9   Jesus cleanses the temple
Ps. 78.2   Prediction of Jesus' use of parables
Ps. 110.1   The divinity of Jesus
Ps. 110.4   The eternal priesthood of Jesus
Ps. 118.22-23   Jesus as the cornerstone
Ps. 118.26   Triumphal entry of Jesus.

Discussion Starters

Do you ever feel that God has forsaken you?

Describe the things that cause you the most pain.

Discuss how Jesus suffered for all of humanity.

Hearing the Word of God

Psalm 22

To the Chief Musician. Set to 'The Deer of the Dawn'.
A Psalm of David.

1 My God, my God, why have You forsaken me?
    Why are You so far from helping me,
    And from the words of my groaning?
2 O my God, I cry in the daytime, but You do not hear;
    And in the night season, and am not silent.
3 But You are holy,
    Enthroned in the praises of Israel.
4 Our fathers trusted in You;
    They trusted, and You delivered them.
5 They cried to You, and were delivered;
    They trusted in You, and were not ashamed.
6 But I am a worm, and no man;
    A reproach of men, and despised by the people.
7 All those who see me ridicule me;
    They shoot out the lip, they shake the head, saying,
8 'He trusted in the LORD, let Him rescue Him;
    Let Him deliver Him, since He delights in Him!'
9 But You are He who took me out of the womb;
    You made me trust while on my mother's breasts.
10 I was cast upon You from birth.
    From my mother's womb You have been my God.
11 Be not far from me, For trouble is near;
    For there is none to help.
12 Many bulls have surrounded me;
    Strong bulls of Bashan have encircled me.
13 They gape at me with their mouths,
    Like a raging and roaring lion.
14 I am poured out like water,
    And all my bones are out of joint;
    My heart is like wax; It has melted within me.
15 My strength is dried up like a potsherd,
    And my tongue clings to my jaws;
    You have brought me to the dust of death.

¹⁶ For dogs have surrounded me;
   The congregation of the wicked has enclosed me.
   They pierced my hands and my feet;
¹⁷ I can count all my bones.
   They look and stare at me.
¹⁸ They divide my garments among them,
   And for my clothing they cast lots.
¹⁹ But You, O LORD, do not be far from me;
   O my Strength, hasten to help me!
²⁰ Deliver me from the sword,
   My precious life from the power of the dog.
²¹ Save me from the lion's mouth
   And from the horns of the wild oxen!
   You have answered me.
²² I will declare Your name to my brethren;
   In the midst of the assembly I will praise You.
²³ You who fear the LORD, praise Him!
   All you descendants of Jacob, glorify Him,
   And fear Him, all you offspring of Israel!
²⁴ For He has not despised nor abhorred
   the affliction of the afflicted;
   Nor has He hidden His face from him;
   But when He cried to him, He heard.
²⁵ My praise shall be of You in the great assembly;
   I will pay my vows before those who fear Him.
²⁶ The poor shall eat and be satisfied;
   Those who seek Him will praise the LORD.
   Let your heart live forever!
²⁷ All the ends of the world
   Shall remember and turn to the LORD,
   And all the families of the nations
   Shall worship before You.
²⁸ For the kingdom is the LORD's,
   And He rules over the nations.
²⁹ All the prosperous of the earth Shall eat and worship;
   All those who go down to the dust Shall bow before Him,
   Even he who cannot keep himself alive.

³⁰ A posterity shall serve Him.
   It will be recounted of the Lord to the next generation,
³¹ They will come and declare His righteousness
   to a people who will be born,
   That He has done this.

Introduction

Psalm 22 follows the same pattern of passionate prayer as Psalm 13. It can be outlined in two parts: the first part is prayer (vv. 1-21a), and the second part is praise (vv. 21b-31). At the end of part one, the psalmist professes his faith, saying, 'You have answered me' (v. 21). We do not know how he comes to that conclusion. We do not know exactly what the process was except that, somehow, in coming to God in prayer and in seeking the Lord, he reaches the conclusion that God has heard his prayer. Even though nothing has changed, the psalmist changes from prayer to praise. As we take a look at this powerful Psalm, we will learn how to experience the presence of God as we move from prayer to praise.

A Psalm of Pain

¹ My God, my God, why have You forsaken me?
   Why are You so far from helping me,
   And from the words of my groaning?
² O my God, I cry in the daytime, but You do not hear;
   And in the night season, and am not silent (Ps. 22.1-2).

Before reaching the place of praise, David expresses his feeling of pain that God has not answered him. David feels forsaken, and he longs to sense God's presence. He knows that God is everywhere present; yet, God has not intervened to help him. Therefore, he feels deserted by God. David is in trouble; yet, God has not delivered him. Consequently, he feels like he has been left to fend for himself. He faces a deep sense of aloneness.

The lamenting cry of David is deep and piercing; yet, it is not a cry of complete despair and hopelessness. He begins his prayer in a way that suggests a longing and yearning to be in the presence of his God. He uses the phrase 'My God, my God'. He is calling upon the God of whom he sings, 'The Lord is my shepherd, I shall not want' (Ps. 23.1). He is crying out to the God who protects him through the 'valley of the shadow of death' and who comforts him with his rod and staff (Ps. 23.4). He is David's provider who 'prepares a table' before him even in the presence of his enemies, who anoints his head with oil, and who makes his cup to run over (Ps. 23.5). David's desire is to live forever in God's presence – to 'dwell in the house of the Lord forever' (Ps. 23.6). When David cries out 'my God, my God', he is seeking divine aid from the God who delivered him from the lion and the bear, who saved him from the mighty Goliath, and who protected him from the armies of the Philistines and from those of Saul. David is pleading with his God, who had brought him from the sheepfold and made him king over Israel.

David's lament to God is not uttered in an attitude of doubt. David does not wonder if God is real or if God is able to help. His prayer is an attempt to convince God to intervene, to act. He is saying to God, 'You have saved me in the past, please save me again now.'

David's prayer anticipates Lk. 18.1, where Jesus 'spoke unto them a parable that men ought always to pray and not faint'; that is, they should not give up on praying. He told the story of a woman whose rights were being violated, and she brought her case to a judge. The judge would not help her, but she continued coming back again and again. Jesus said something like this, 'I tell you what this unjust judge will do, he cares not about this woman or her need, but because of her persistence, he will do what she asks'. Jesus then said, 'how much more should your father in heaven, who loves you, and cares for you, answer the prayer of the one who calls upon him. I tell you he will answer them quickly' (Lk. 18.1-8). David is praying this kind of persistent prayer. And it is this kind of persistent and urgent prayer that God hears and answers.

We might also point to the desperate woman who asked Jesus to heal her daughter who was possessed by an evil spirit. The disciples told her to be quiet. They told her that she was not a Jew and that she should leave Jesus alone. They said, 'You are a Gentile, and we don't minister to your kind'; but she kept crying out, and finally, Jesus asked, 'What do you want?' She replied, 'My daughter is grievously vexed with a devil'. And he said, 'Go your way; your daughter is healed'. Then, he turned to his disciples and he said, 'I have not seen so great faith, no not in Israel' (Mt. 15.22-28). It was because of her persistence that Jesus stood still and turned and answered her prayer.

God pays attention to people who will cry out to him from the midst of their pain.

God had not answered, but David continued to pray in the daytime and in the nighttime. He did not give up hope. When we are in trouble and God has not delivered us, do we continue to pray? Do we cry out to God night and day for his help, or do we only spend our time complaining to our friends and family. Friends and family are important as support and as encouragers, but only God can deliver us. If we have not been crying out to God in the daytime and in the nighttime, then we cannot expect God to act.

A Psalm of Remembrance

> ³ **But You are holy,**
>   **Enthroned in the praises of Israel.**
> ⁴ **Our fathers trusted in You;**
>   **They trusted, and You delivered them.**
> ⁵ **They cried to You, and were delivered;**
>   **They trusted in You, and were not ashamed (Ps. 22.3-5).**

Here in verses 3-5, David looks back to the testimonies of his ancestors in the faith. The psalmist is crying out around-the-clock, and then he remembers what God has done for his father, for his mother, and for his people.

David is feeling abandoned, and it seems that his prayer has not been heard. Nevertheless, without wavering, he continues to affirm the holy character of God. The delay in the answer of David's prayers is not due to a lack of goodness or righteousness on God's part, for God is holy. Furthermore, David's feelings of abandonment are not due to God's impotence, for God is Israel's king, who sits enthroned on the praises of Israel. Verse 3, which is often quoted in the church, proclaims that the holy God inhabits the praises of his people Israel.

We remember from Psalm 13 that the psalms of lament almost always have a reference to trust, and we notice that the theme of trust is repeated here in Ps. 22.4-5. David says, 'Our fathers trusted in you, and you delivered. They cried and were delivered. They trusted and they were not ashamed'. In effect, the psalmist says, 'Now I am trusting God. I am trusting as my ancestors trusted, and I expect to have the same response to my prayers.'

A Psalm of Opposition

> 6 But I am a worm, and no man;
>   A reproach of men, and despised by the people.
> ⁷ All those who see me ridicule me;
>   They shoot out the lip, they shake the head, saying,
> ⁸ 'He trusted in the LORD, let Him rescue him;
>   Let Him deliver him, since He delights in him!'
>   (Ps. 22.6-8).

After his expression of trust in the Lord, David restates his problem. It seems that he is surrounded by opposition and oppressed by persecutors. We do not know the identity of the psalmist's opposition, but he is clearly facing desertion not only from God but also from the people around him. He says, 'I am a worm, I am a reproach; I am despised; I am ridiculed'. Here is a person who is rejected. The psalmist is remembering what God has done in the past. God saved his people; God has answered prayer. Nonetheless, the people who should come to his aid are not helping him; instead, they are abusing him. He is alone in the midst of a crowd. No one is helping David, and in fact, everyone is ridiculing him. We all feel like that at times – alone in the midst of a crowd. We attend church, but feel isolated, discouraged, despondent, with no one to help.

David's plight reminds us of Job, whose friends should have been encouraging him and praying for him; but instead, they are accusing him. They say, 'if you had been a good man, these tragedies would never have happened to you. Surely, you must have sinned against God, and he is punishing you.' This kind of judgmental behavior continues to happen in the church. Christians who are suffering from sickness or tragedy are often accused of bringing the trouble upon themselves by their unbelief or by their disobedience. Nevertheless, faithful and dedicated Christians are subject to sickness and suffering just like everyone else.

A Psalm of Trust

> ⁹ But You are He who took me out of the womb;
>   You made me trust while on my mother's breasts.
> ¹⁰ I was cast upon You from birth.
>   From my mother's womb You have been my God
>   (Ps. 22.9-10).

In the face of ridicule and opposition, the psalmist recalls the grace of God in earlier days. David declares that he has served God all the days of his life. David claims that God has cared for him from his mother's womb. Then, after he was born, when he was nursing at his mother's breasts, the Lord cared for him. Therefore, from birth God has been a reality in his life. God has been with him and has provided for him.

A Psalm of Dangers

In verses 11-13, the psalmist again sets forth his desperate situation. Many enemies are circling around him, and he compares his opposers to animals. He prays for God's help saying,

> ¹¹ Be not far from me, For trouble is near;
>   For there is none to help.
> ¹² Many bulls have surrounded me;
>   Strong bulls of Bashan have encircled me.
> ¹³ They gape at me with their mouths,
>   Like a raging and roaring lion (Ps. 22.11-13).

His enemies are so dreadful that they are like animals. They are like angry, ravenous beasts. He pleads with God saying, 'Be not far from me, for trouble is near, and there is none to help.' David's God seems far off, but his trouble is close at hand, and he needs help. Who are these enemies? They are bulls and they are lions. Angry people are encircling him like strong bulls. Also, like lions, ravenous people are gaping and roaring at him with their mouths.

A Psalm of Suffering

Not only is David surrounded by danger, but his body itself is deteriorating rapidly. He is so sick and so afflicted that he feels like his whole life is falling apart. He reveals his pain by saying,

> ¹⁴ I am poured out like water,
>   And all my bones are out of joint;
>   My heart is like wax; It has melted within me.
> ¹⁵ My strength is dried up like a potsherd,
>   And my tongue clings to my jaws;
>   You have brought me to the dust of death (Ps. 22.14-15).

We do not know if David was physically ill or if his references to illness are metaphors that signify the painful effects of the opposition that he is facing. Sometimes we may not be physically ill, but emotionally we feel like we could die. We feel sick, because we are dealing with something that is draining and devastating.

So the psalmist says, 'I am poured out like water'. It is as if his energy, his life force, is being drained. Have you ever received a troubling phone call or experienced the news of a disaster, and you seem to feel your life draining from your body?

The psalmist adds, 'all of my bones are out of joint; my heart is like wax; my strength is dried up; my tongue sticks to my jaws; you have brought me to the dust of death.' David feels like he is dying – his strength is exhausted and his life is fading away. He feels like a discarded, broken piece of clay pottery ('a potsherd').

A Psalm of Rejection

And then, those that are around are just talking about what will happen when he dies.

> ¹⁶ **For dogs have surrounded me;**
> **The assembly of the wicked has enclosed me.**
> **They pierced my hands and my feet;**
> ¹⁷ **I can count all my bones.**
> **They look and stare at me.**
> ¹⁸ **They divide my garments among them,**
> **And for my clothing they cast lots (Ps. 22.16-18).**

'Dogs have surrounded me', he says. First it was bulls, then lions, now dogs. These dogs are 'an assembly of the wicked'. After circling around him, these dogs have pierced his hands and his feet. In the original context of the Psalm, the meaning would be that the dogs are biting David's hands and feet. Their long fangs are piercing through the flesh. The writer of Matthew's Gospel sees this verse fulfilled at the cross when the hands and feet of Jesus were pierced by the nails.

The acuteness of the psalmist's condition is pressed further by his statement 'I can count all my bones.' It seems that his body has wasted away because of illness or because he has been unable to procure food. For whatever reason, however, he is nothing but skin and bones.

Onlookers stand by awaiting his death. In anticipation of his approaching demise, they begin to divide up his garments among themselves, and they cast lots for his clothing. These gawkers would not be members of his family, because the family would follow established guidelines for dispensing of the deceased's personal property. Again, the Gospel of Matthew picks up this psalm and applies it to Jesus. As Jesus died upon the cross, the Roman soldiers who had carried out the death sentence of crucifixion cast lots for his seamless robe.

A Psalm of Prayer

While David's enemies are circling around him and waiting for him to die and wondering how they can profit from his death, David chooses to turn his gaze away from his enemies and back toward God. Even when facing desperate circumstances, believers can choose where to focus their attention. The psalmist chooses to focus again upon God and to cry out in prayer. Pleading for divine intervention, his prayer is this:

> [19] **But You, O LORD, do not be far from me;**
>   **O my Strength, hasten to help me!**
> [20] **Deliver me from the sword,**
>   **My precious life from the power of the dog.**
> [21] **Save me from the lion's mouth**
>   **And from the horns of the wild oxen!**
>   **You have answered me (Ps. 22.19-21).**

The psalmist has painted a gruesome picture of his critical situation. And now, he puts into words an urgent petition, a pointed prayer. His request is 'O Lord, do not be far from me, O my strength. Hasten to help me.' Knowing that his end is near at hand, David urges God to hurry. There is no time to lose. The situation is looking hopeless, and he needs God to intervene immediately. He prays that God will deliver him from the power of the sword and of the dog. He asks that God will save him from the lion's mouth and from the horns of the wild oxen. The animals spoken of here are a repetition from the previous verses, but here they are in reverse order.

David then makes an amazing statement at the end of verse 21. He proclaims, 'You have answered me.' Suddenly, David lays claim to

God's promises and declares his assurance that God has heard his prayer.

A Psalm of Promise

David's assurance that God has heard his prayer moves him to make two promises. First, he promises to testify to his brethren. Second, he promises to offer a thanksgiving sacrifice in the temple. These two promises are really just two parts of one event. When David comes to the temple to offer his sacrifice of praise, he will share his testimony of how God brought him out of trouble.

> ²² I will declare Your name to my brethren;
>   In the midst of the assembly I will praise You.
> ²³ You who fear the LORD, praise Him!
>   'All you descendants of Jacob, glorify Him,
>   And fear Him, all you offspring of Israel!
> ²⁴ For He has not despised nor abhorred
>   the affliction of the afflicted;
>   Nor has He hidden His face from Him;
>   But when He cried to Him, He heard.
> ²⁵ My praise shall be of You in the great assembly;
>   I will pay my vows before those who fear Him.
> ²⁶ The poor shall eat and be satisfied;
>   Those who seek Him will praise the LORD.
>   Let your heart live forever! (Ps. 22.22-26)

Not only does David promise to praise the Lord, but he also calls upon the people to offer up praise. He invites the people saying, 'all of you who fear the Lord, praise him, praise him.' Is the psalmist saying that they should praise God because things are better now? No, David's situation is not yet better. Is he asking the people to praise God because the trouble is over? No, the trouble is not over yet. Instead, David is urging the people to praise God because he knows that God has heard his prayer. God has the answer, and he is on the way to intervene and to deliver. A similar perspective is stated in the New Testament by John, who says, 'if we know that He hears us, whatever we ask, we know that we have the petitions that we have asked of Him' (1 Jn 5.15). Both David and John understood the truth that when we pray in faith, God responds. So the psalmist declares, 'I believe that God has heard my prayer, so let us praise him!'

But praying in faith is not so simple as it sounds. To pray with faith demands more than simply repeating a Scripture promise over and over. It requires more than words and confessions and making claims upon God. The process of finding assurance in prayer is what many of us have called 'praying through'. This process is difficult to explain, and it is difficult to learn. The best way to learn how to pray through is to spend time praying alongside a person who is experienced in the process. We must learn from them, and we must follow their example. To pray through like David prayed means that we pour out our hearts to God and express honestly our deepest needs. It means that we cry out for God's help. It means that we look back and remember what God has done in the past, and it means that we express our trust in God for the present time.

To pray through means that we wrestle with God like Jacob and that we refuse to let go of God until he promises to deliver us. Somewhere during this process, the Holy Spirit works in our hearts to give us an assurance that God has heard our prayers. That assurance can materialize in many different ways. Most of the time it presents as a feeling of peace that comes over us. There might be times when we open up the Bible and read a verse and we know that this verse is meant for us. With a still small voice, God might speak to us in our minds. We may have a dream, or we may receive another kind of miraculous sign. There are many different ways that God speaks to us to give us that assurance.

Psalm 22 holds together that tension between crying out to God in prayer and praising God for the answer. In our worship, we must choose which approach to take. Psalm 22 actually teaches us that we must do both. We must pray with urgency, with passion, with determination, and with faith. We must also, after we have prayed, express our trust in God and offer up to him a sacrifice of praise. Often if we begin with prayer our worship flows into praise.

Notice the last line where the psalmist says, 'I will pay my vows'. In biblical times people often made vows to God in hopes that they would move him to hear their petitions. For example, we read in the Psalms that the psalmists would make a vow to offer a sacrifice. They would say to God, 'When you have answered my prayer I will come to the temple and offer up a sacrifice of praise'. This sacrifice of praise is a called a thanksgiving offering (Lev. 7.13-15).

A Psalm of Praise

When David moves from prayer to praise, he first focuses upon his own praise. He promises to praise God with a sacrifice. Then he calls upon the congregation to give praise to God. In verse 27, he also expands his call to all inhabitants of the earth. He invites everyone to join in with him, saying,

> ²⁷ All the ends of the world
>   Shall remember and turn to the LORD,
>   And all the families of the nations
>   Shall worship before You.
> ²⁸ For the kingdom is the LORD's,
>   And He rules over the nations.
> ²⁹ All the prosperous of the earth shall eat and worship;
>   All those who go down to the dust
>   shall bow before Him,
>   Even he who cannot keep himself alive.
> ³⁰ A posterity shall serve Him.
>   It will be recounted of the Lord
>   to the next generation,
> ³¹ They will come and declare His righteousness
>   to a people who will be born,
>   That He has done this (Ps. 22.27-31).

David declares that the entire world, to the 'ends of the earth', will turn to the Lord; all the 'families of the nations' will worship the Lord. The reason that the people of the nations will come to worship God is that the 'kingdom is the Lord's'. The Lord rules over the nations. Those who are alive and prospering will worship God, and even those who have died will bow down before him. David's words foreshadow the claims of the Apostle Paul, who writes, 'every knee shall bow ... and every tongue shall confess' (Philippians 2.10-11).

Looking into the future, David sees that even after we die, our posterity, our children, our descendants will serve God (v. 30). The next generation will declare his righteousness to a people yet to be born. Generation after generation will be hearing about the works of the Lord.

The psalmist concludes Psalm 22 with the powerful affirmation that the coming generations will know that it is the Lord who has been at work in our lives – 'He has done this'. God has done this.

David promises to testify and to tell other generations what God has done. Some of us have grown up in Christian families and have grown up in church, yet still we may not have heard the testimonies of the mighty works of God. Sadly, we often focus so much on the present that we forget to tell our children and grandchildren what God has done for us in the past. It is God's works from the past that provide a foundation for the future.

In my family, and the church where I grew up, there was no emphasis on testimony; and I did not know the stories of the past. My parents and grandparents were Christians, but I never heard of any great works that God had done in their lives. In fact, my grandfather was a Baptist preacher, but I know nothing about the events of his ministry.

My grandmother was more talkative, but she rarely spoke of spiritual things. I finally caught a glimpse of her faith when she was about 90 years old (she lived to be 105). I went to visit her, and she offered to make lunch (I loved her biscuits). We were standing in the kitchen; she was sifting her flour, and we were talking. She began to speak to me in a whisper, almost as if she were telling me a deep secret that she was afraid to make known. She said to me,

> I know that your church believes in praying for the sick, but we never did that. But I will tell you something that I've never told anybody else. When I was a little girl, I was 12 years old, and my mother got sick, and everybody said she was going to die. She was lying in the bed, dying, and all the family had gone to bed; and we were waiting on mama to die. I got up out of the bed and I went down to mama's room, and I knelt down beside her bed. I began to pray, and I said Jesus, I've been told that you don't work miracles anymore, but I need a miracle today. If you are real, then please heal my mama. And I don't know if it was my prayer or something else, but Mama was healed and she was able to get out of bed and she fully recovered.

As I reflect upon my grandmother's story, I would note that it reports a marvelous miracle of God's healing power. Moreover, I wonder why my family, my grandmother in particular, did not realize how valuable the story could be. We need to tell our children what God has done for us. We need to tell new Christians the wonderful works of God. We need to tell those who are young and old, 'this is what the Lord has done'.

The Jews continue to observe the Passover in order to share from generation to generation the experience of the exodus from Egypt. The church continues to celebrate the Lord's Supper in order to re-experience the atoning death of Jesus on the cross. The Lord's Supper is a way of reminding everyone that Jesus died on the cross and that his blood is still efficacious for the forgiveness of sins. The bread is the body of Christ, and the wine is the blood of Christ. Beyond these rituals, we should regularly report to our children what God has done in our personal lives. Through our testimonies, they learn that God is real; and as they grow up, they will be strengthened as they rely upon the testimonies of their elders.

Psalm 22 and the Cross of Christ

Psalm 22 is appropriate for any believer, at any time in history from David until now. Like David, we can approach God in our times of pain and call upon him saying, 'God I need your help. I am surrounded; I feel like I am dying; I feel like I need you Lord. My life is falling apart; and I need you to help me.' This Psalm is appropriate for the faithful, for God's people who are suffering.

And that is why Jesus appropriated Ps. 22.1 for himself – it reflects the depth of despair and suffering that he endured upon the cross. The Gospel of Mark reports that Jesus, while hanging upon the cross, uttered the words of the psalmist: 'My God, my God, why have you forsaken me?' (Mk 15.34). Jesus, knowing the Scriptures from the Old Testament, is able to take this verse and apply it to the suffering that he is going through.

When Jesus says, 'My God, my God, why have you forsaken me?', he is not asking for information. It is a rhetorical question that is meant not to require an answer. The question is an expression of pain. The word 'Why?' is a way of asking God to reveal his presence. Jesus is not really asking, 'Why?' He knew why. He knew the reason. It is *not* a question of asking for information, it *is* the expression of suffering that identifies with the psalmist David. Jesus, the son of David, appropriates the words of David, laying claim to the Scripture that was written hundreds of years before. Later, the disciples of

Jesus look back to Psalm 22, and they see other correspondences between the words of the psalm and the events of the crucifixion. Like David, Jesus was surrounded by enemies and suffered rejection by his people.

When Jesus quotes Ps. 22.1, he expresses the awful reality of the cross. Jesus was not imagining the pain. It was genuine. It was real suffering. He was really dying. His life was really going out of him. His heart was really breaking. His bones were really showing. It was real. It was not imaginary. Jesus identifies with his people who had suffered in the past and who had sung this psalm for hundreds of years.

Also, this psalm punctuates for us how the cross was an indictment of the sin of humanity. Jesus is surrounded by his own people, the Jews who rejected him. They turned against him, and his affliction is because of the sin of humanity. On the cross, he is bearing the total sin and rebellion of all humanity. Here in the center of Psalm 22, in verses 11 through 18, we read about the rejection of the people. There are also powerful forces at work in first-century Judea, all attempting to destroy Jesus: the governor, Herod, the Sanhedrin court, the ruling Jews, and the religious people. These people are attacking Jesus, while they should be supporting him.

It is easy to connect verses 9 and 10 to the life of Jesus as well. From birth, from his mother's womb, he trusted God. When choosing the mother who would bear his son, God found a humble woman who trusted the Lord. Jesus, the Son of God, was taught and nurtured by a young woman named Mary. She taught him to trust in the Lord. Along with his earthly father Joseph, they together created a loving environment for Jesus to grow.

Why did Jesus quote from Psalm 22? One reason was to bring that Psalm to all those who were listening to him around the cross and to all of us who would read the Gospels. When he quoted from Psalm 22, he brought the psalm to the people, because even in his death, Jesus had in mind the people who were and would be listening. He even cared about the thief that was beside him on the other cross as well. One of his last words was 'Father forgive them for they know not what they do'. Jesus did not go to the cross feeling sorry for himself; rather, he went to the cross out of love for lost humanity. He spoke the words of Psalm 22 in order to say to us, 'This Psalm points to me'. His quotation of Psalm 22 suggests that everything that happened in Psalm 22 was happening on the cross, and we are *all* witnesses.

Connecting with the Psalm

(Questions for discussion)

Discuss the need to pray persistently, passionately, but humbly?

What are some ways that you have experienced opposition? How should we pray against opposition?

Identify what the psalmist is feeling and experiencing. Have you experienced the same feelings?

What do you see as the main point of this psalm?

How does this psalm guide you in your prayers?

What if … ?

(Creative and imaginative ideas)

What if we obey Jesus by praying for our enemies?

What if we choose to state our trust in God even when everything seems to be going against us?

What if we reach out to other people who are suffering and pray for them?

Now, come up with your own 'What if … ?'

4

THE PASSIONATE PURSUIT OF TRUST IN GOD: PSALM 27

Setting the Direction

How important is our trust in God? In light of the uncertainties surrounding us in the contemporary world, Christians must learn to put their complete trust in God and in his grace. The world economy is in shambles; terrorism continues to threaten any hopes for global peace; new drug-resistant diseases endanger our health; and frequent natural disasters challenge our ability to maintain a stable and effective society. It is only natural that non-Christians will be pessimistic, suspicious, and skeptical, but Christians must rise to the occasion and confess their trust in God. God has not vacated his throne, and he has not been stripped of his sovereignty. To trust God means that we accept God at his word and that we put ourselves unreservedly into his hands.

Faith is the basis of our salvation – we are saved by grace 'through faith' (Eph. 2.8-9), but faith is also a necessary ingredient in our ongoing relationship with God. As Pentecostals, we are tempted think of faith as the ability to do something great – to perform a miracle, to move mountains, to accomplish something spectacular. However, there is another kind of biblical faith, the kind exemplified in Psalm 27. It is the faith of constant trust, the faith in God that stands fast when we are under attack from the enemy. When we are surrounded, faith says, 'I will believe the Lord no matter what is happening. I will trust God.' This faith is a kind of constancy, a kind of firmness, a kind of steadfastness. It is the kind of trust in God that Paul is talking about when he says to the Corinthians, 'Be steadfast, immovable, always abounding in the work of the Lord, knowing that your labor is not in vain in the Lord' (1 Cor. 15.58). It is the kind of trust that is exemplified in Paul's own life when he says,

> We are troubled on every side but not distressed,
> perplexed but not in despair,
> persecuted but not forsaken,
> cast down but not destroyed (2 Cor. 4.8-9).

How can we maintain this level of hope? Hope like Paul's is possible only when we are trusting in the Lord. This kind of trust is what the writer of Hebrews 11 is talking about when he declares,

> By faith Abel offered up to God a more excellent sacrifice than Cain … By faith Noah built the ark, and he saved his family … By faith Abraham went out to the land that God gave him, even though he did not know where he was going … By faith Moses left Egypt and chose to be with God's people rather than to enjoy the pleasures of sin temporarily … By faith the walls of Jericho fell down.

The heroes of Hebrews 11 were regular people who trusted God in the midst of difficult circumstances and in the midst of challenging times. They were not always appreciated, applauded, or supported by their contemporaries. More often, they were ridiculed, persecuted, and judged to be mentally unstable.

Like the spiritual heroes of Hebrews 11, we are living in perilous times; but it is in these times that we should trust God and believe that he will do something great through us. It is when our society is in deep trouble that we Christians must stand up in faith and demonstrate that we trust God. In so doing, we will be like a light on the hilltop, like a candle in the darkness. Let us be a witness to God's goodness.

Given the battles that we fight today, the opposition that we face, and the challenges that are before us, we must maintain the same attitude of trust that is exemplified in Psalm 27. Trust in God is vital to our survival. It is essential that God's people learn to trust God. We need to realize and understand that no matter what goes on in the economy, we can trust the Lord to be our provider. Whatever goes on in the government, we can trust the Lord to be our guide. Whatever goes on in our community, we can trust in the Lord to be our protection. Whatever goes on with our health, we can trust that the Lord is our healer. No matter what goes on with our family or on our job, we can trust in the Lord to be our strength. We do not trust in what humans can do. We do not trust in what the government can do for us or what our employer can do for us. We must learn to trust in the Lord, and that trust cannot be diverted by circumstances.

Discussion Starters

Are there times when you find it difficult to trust God?

How do you normally react to bad news?

How are you affected by people around you who constantly express doubts, fears, and anxieties?

Share one or more of your favorite Scripture verses about trusting in God.

Hearing the Word of God

Psalm 27

A Psalm of David.

[1] The LORD is my light and my salvation;
　　Whom shall I fear?
　　The LORD is the strength of my life;
　　Of whom shall I be afraid?
[2] When the wicked came against me to eat up my flesh,
　　My enemies and foes, they stumbled and fell.
[3] Though an army may encamp against me,
　　My heart shall not fear;
　　Though war should rise against me,
　　I am trusting in this.
[4] One thing I have desired of the LORD, that will I seek:
　　That I may dwell in the house of the LORD
　　All the days of my life,
　　To behold the beauty of the LORD,
　　And to inquire in His temple.
[5] For in the time of trouble
　　He shall hide me in His pavilion;
　　In the secret place of His tabernacle
　　　He shall hide me;
　　He shall set me high upon a rock.
[6] And now my head shall be lifted up
　　above my enemies all around me;
　　Therefore I will offer sacrifices of joy
　　　in His tabernacle;
　　I will sing, yes, I will sing praises to the LORD.
[7] Hear, O LORD, when I cry with my voice!
　　Have mercy also upon me, and answer me.
[8] When You said, 'Seek My face,'
　　My heart said to You, 'Your face, LORD, I will seek.'
[9] Do not hide Your face from me;
　　Do not turn Your servant away in anger;
　　You have been my help;
　　Do not leave me nor forsake me,
　　　O God of my salvation.
[10] When my father and my mother forsake me,

Then the LORD will take care of me.
¹¹ Teach me Your way, O LORD,
   And lead me in a smooth path,
      because of my enemies.
¹² Do not deliver me to the will of my adversaries;
   For false witnesses have risen against me,
   And such as breathe out violence.
¹³ I would have lost heart, unless I had believed
   That I would see the goodness of the LORD
   In the land of the living.
¹⁴ Wait on the LORD; be of good courage,
   And He shall strengthen your heart;
   Wait, I say, on the LORD!

Introduction to the Psalms of Trust

When we think of the Psalms, we usually think of praise, but there are many kinds of Psalms. The most common type of psalm is the psalm of prayer, also called the lament, in which the psalmist is encountering some form of trouble. In the laments, the psalmist needs help from God; and he calls upon God. He cries out to God for his help. The psalms of urgent prayer are the most common type of psalm within the book of Psalms. In the midst of praying and in the midst of crying out to God, the psalmists would come to a place where they profess complete trust in the Lord. Even though the storm is still raging, the psalmist declares, 'I will trust in the Lord'. Even though the waters continue to rise, he says, 'I will trust in the Lord'. Even though the enemy has come against him, he insists, 'I will trust in the Lord'. It is that complete trust, that unwavering faith, that sustains the psalmist in the time of need. He grasps hold of God to find safety in the midst of the storm.

I am reminded of the old song that says,

Till the storm passes over,
   till the thunder sounds no more,
   till the clouds roll forever from the sky,
Hold me fast, let me stand,
   in the hollow of your hand,
Keep me safe till the storm passes by.

When the storm is raging, we must hold fast to the anchor, Jesus Christ. He is the anchor of our soul. We must hold fast to him and keep our trust in him. The Psalms do not tell us to trust in the Lord only when things are going well. Genuine trust in the Lord is active when things are not going well, yet we have determined in our hearts that what our eyes see and what our heart feels is not everything. The future is not determined by our senses or by our circumstances. Our future is in the hands of God. He is working behind the scenes, and we must put our trust in him.

The profession of trust is an important element in the psalms of lament. The following psalms of lament include a brief statement of trust in the Lord.

'… put your trust in the LORD' (Ps. 4.5).

'let all those who put their trust in you rejoice' (Ps. 5.11).

'O LORD my God, in you do I put my trust' (Ps. 7.1).

'but I have trusted in your mercy' (Ps. 13.5).

'O you who save by your right hand them which put their trust in you' (Ps. 17.7).

'Our fathers trusted in you: they trusted, and you delivered them' (Ps. 22.4).

These and many other examples demonstrate that the confession of trust is an important element within the prayer psalms. The profession of trust, which is no more than a single statement in many psalms, is expanded in Psalm 27 to fill the entire psalm. Thus, the confession of trust is transformed from its role as one small part of the lament psalm to create a new type of psalm, the psalm of trust.

Unlike the psalms of lament, Psalm 27 is not uttered during a time of suffering. The psalmist does not express a specific need. His only prayer is for the continuation of God's presence in his life. Furthermore, he does not come to God with a specific item of thanksgiving. That is, he does not point back to a particular event for which he is giving thanks. Many of the psalms focus on one thing for which the psalmist gives thanks or praise, one act of deliverance, or one event in the life of the psalmist. Many of the psalms focus on giving praise for the exodus deliverance; others praise God for his role as creator, or for his role as king. But this psalm, Psalm 27, does not have a focus on prayer or praise. This psalm focuses on trust and faith. In it the psalmist says, 'In whatever situation I find myself, I have determined that I will trust in the Lord'.

Psalm 27

Who is God?

At the heart of this psalm is a deep theology of worship. Many Christians do not have a very good opinion of theologians or of theology, and one reason for this negative opinion of theology is that theologians talk in a language that only they understand. The Psalms are Israel's theology, but they present theology in a different kind of language. Prayer and worship are deeply theological – they reflect our most earnest beliefs about God. Therefore, the Psalms are the theology of the people, and they display theology that emerges from a personal relationship with God. The writers of the Psalms express the importance of God for their own lives and for the life of their congregation. Psalm 27.1 says,

> ¹The LORD is my light and my salvation;
>   Whom shall I fear?
> The LORD is the strength of my life;
>   Of whom shall I be afraid?

'The Lord is…' – this is a statement of theology. When we attempt to describe God, we are expressing our theology. Unlike traditional theology, which describes God in abstract philosophical terms, the Psalms use concrete images. A theologian might say that God is 'eternally existent, self-sufficient, omnipotent, omniscient, and omnipresent.' But David says, 'The Lord is my light and my salvation'. Is God eternal? Of course, but he is our light. Is God omniscient? Of course, but he is our salvation. Is God omnipresent? Of course, but he is the strength of our lives. When it is dark and we need a light, the Lord is our light. When we cannot see the path in front of us, he shines the light on our pathway. The Lord is our light. The Lord is our salvation. When we are in trouble, he saves us. When we have a need, he delivers us. The Lord is our light, and the Lord is our salvation. The Lord is the strength of our lives. When we are weak, in him we are strong. When we are facing a Goliath in our lives, we can turn to the strength of the Lord, and we can say to the giant, 'You come against me with a sword and with a spear, but I come to you in the name of the Lord of hosts.' 'The Lord is the strength of my life, of whom shall I be afraid?' The Psalms are deeply theological, but the theology of the Psalms is expressed in the language of worship and in the language of the common person.

God is the Strength of Those Who Trust Him.

When David says, 'The Lord is my light', he is making a theological statement. When he says, 'The Lord is the strength of my life, of whom shall I be afraid', he is constructing and confessing his theology. And in making the confession, he is worshiping God in his theology. David's theology is a theology of worship and a theology of praise. He is making a statement about his beliefs in God.

Psalm 27 is a very personal statement and creed: the psalmist uses the word 'my' – 'the Lord is *my* light'. Of course, we all know that God rules as the God of the universe and that he is Lord over everyone, but we must lay claim to him as our God. When David uses the personal phrase, 'my' light, he is not making an abstract statement that indicates a vague belief in God. Even the demons believe and tremble (Jas 2.19). David's belief is not vague and abstract; his belief is personal; his faith is real; and his theology is relational.

Like David, we can say 'The Lord is *my* light', because he is a personal God. In Psalm 23, David declares, 'The Lord is *my* shepherd, I shall not want. He makes *me* lie down in green pastures. He leads *me* beside the still waters. He restores *my* soul' (Ps. 23.1-3). If we could ever fully comprehend the depth of God's love and the personal nature of his relationship with us, it would transform our lives. God is a God who cares deeply for you and for me individually. God is not satisfied that we have a general belief in the existence of God; rather, he wants to be our covenant God. He wants to be our savior. We have a very personal relationship with God. We are his 'people and the sheep of his pasture' (Ps. 100.3). He has called us by name (Isa. 43.1). He belongs to us, and we belong to him. We can trust him. We can trust him to be our life, our light, our salvation, our strength, our healer, our helper, and our song.

> [2] When the wicked came against me to eat up my flesh,
>   My enemies and foes, they stumbled and fell.
> [3] Though an army may encamp against me,
>   My heart shall not fear;

Though war should rise against me,
I am trusting in this.

In verse two, the psalmist proclaims that he is trusting God to be his strength. He is trusting God to be his safety, even when he is surrounded. He is believing that God will be his security when the enemy comes against him.

Perhaps Peter was thinking of this verse when he wrote, 'Satan, as a roaring lion, goes about seeking whom he may devour' (1 Pet. 5.8). The enemy is seeking to devour us, to destroy us, to wipe us out. However, the psalmist said that when the enemy – the wicked – came upon him to consume him and to devour him, they stumbled and fell. The enemy is pursuing us; but if we resist the devil, he will flee from us. He will stumble, and he will fall. Paul tells the Roman Christians, 'The God of peace will soon crush Satan under your feet' (Rom. 16.20).

In Ps. 27.3, the psalmist adds, 'even though an army should encamp against me, my heart shall not fear; though war should rise against me, I am trusting in this.' Even if we look out and there is an entire army surrounding us, God will protect us; he will make a way.

When the armies of the Assyrians surrounded Jerusalem, King Hezekiah went to the Lord in prayer; and God sent an angel to destroy the armies. Hezekiah admitted to God that the armies of the enemy were invincible and that he needed God's help. He prayed earnestly, 'Save us; help us; deliver us'. That night, the angel of the Lord came down into the camp of the Assyrians and killed 186,000 enemy soldiers. One angel is sufficient to destroy all the enemies that surround us. We read in Ps. 34.7 that the 'angel of the Lord encamps around about those that fear him to deliver them'. In the book of Revelation, we see an angel with a chain in his hand who is coming down to bind the devil and to cast him into the bottomless pit. The Scripture says, 'he laid hold of the dragon, that serpent of old, who is the devil and Satan, and bound him' (Rev. 20.1). We think of the devil as a powerful enemy who has wrought havoc in the midst of the earth and against the church, but it requires only one angel to bind him and to cast him into the bottomless pit.

When an army comes against us, God can deliver us. Sometimes we realize that our task is beyond our abilities, and the opposition is too strong. We may ask, 'How can I overcome this? How can I get over this? How can I deal with this?' Perhaps our problems and troubles are so big that we completely lose hope. How can we deal with these impossible situations? How can we solve these problems? What can we do? The answer is to put our trust in the Lord. He is our light; he is our salvation; and he is our strength. He is the strength of those who trust in him.

God is a Shelter for Those Who Worship Him.
One way that the Lord protects those who trust in him is to hide them in his shelter. He is a refuge to those that worship him. David declares his passion for worship:

> ⁴ **One thing I have desired of the LORD, That will I seek:**
>   **That I may dwell in the house of the LORD**
>   **All the days of my life,**
>   **To behold the beauty of the LORD,**
>   **And to inquire in His temple.**
> ⁵ **For in the time of trouble**
>   **He shall hide me in His pavilion;**
>   **In the secret place of His tabernacle**
>   **He shall hide me;**
>   **He shall set me high upon a rock.**
> ⁶ **And now my head shall be lifted up**
>   **above my enemies all around me;**
>   **Therefore I will offer sacrifices of joy**
>   **in His tabernacle;**
>   **I will sing, yes, I will sing praises to the LORD**
>   **(Ps. 27.4-6).**

The deepest desire of God's people is to dwell in the house of the Lord. The same sentiment is found in Ps. 23.6, where David announces, 'I will dwell in the house of the Lord forever' and in Psalm 84, where we read,

> ¹ How lovely is Your tabernacle,
>   O LORD of hosts!
> ² My soul longs, yes, even faints
>   For the courts of the LORD; ...
> ⁴ Blessed are those who dwell in Your house;
>   They will still be praising You ...
> ¹⁰ For a day in Your courts is better than a thousand.

> I would rather be a doorkeeper in the
>   house of my God
> Than dwell in the tents of wickedness.

The psalmist prays that he might dwell in the house of the Lord all the days of his life, to 'behold the beauty of the Lord, and to inquire in his temple'. His statement indicates that the worship of God is his greatest joy. To dwell in the house of the Lord means to live there and to remain there at all times. To behold the beauty of the Lord means to see God in all his glory. 'Blessed are the pure in heart for they shall see God' (Mt. 5.8).

The one thing that David especially desires is to be in the house of God. It is there among the people of God that David can enjoy the Lord's presence, behold the Lord's beauty, and seek God's face. To be in the house of God is his constant passion; it is the goal and object of his life. Similarly, the early church exhibited a deep desire for constant worship and prayer. Luke reports that the early believers who were newly filled with the spirit continued 'with one accord in the Temple' (Acts 2.46).

In his role as king of Israel, David would have faced any number of daily challenges that would have occupied his time. Nevertheless, he chose to make attendance to the house of God one of his highest priorities. David's example should encourage us to evaluate our own priorities. In our technological age, we are tempted to relegate the house of God to an afterthought while we busily pursue entertainment, pleasure, and affluence.

History teaches us that a passion for the house of God is a characteristic of revival and spiritual vitality. When God's people are spiritually alert, they do not become weary of assembling together to worship the Lord. But when believers consider it a burden to attend services of worship, it is a clear sign of backsliding.

David's desire to be literally *always* in the house of God is, of course, not humanly possible. Therefore, if we are to be always in the presence of God, we must worship wherever we may find ourselves. We must 'rejoice in the Lord always' (Phil. 4.4). Sometimes we think of worship as an activity that is confined to church services, where we have praise and worship, a sermon, prayers, and then we go home. Afterwards, we say that we have worshiped. However, for God's people, worship is a way of life; and to dwell in the house of the Lord represents continual worship. We worship daily and continually. On Monday morning, we arise; and, through the Spirit, we make the house of the Lord our dwelling place. Our home should be the house of the Lord. When we drive our car, we should make it the house of the Lord – a place of worship. When we are on our jobs, we should make that location a sanctuary of God. Wherever we happen to be, we can lift our voices in praise to God. God wants to be present with us at all times and in all places. We must fellowship with him and commune with him at all times. We must practice the presence of God. For the Christian, God is always present; and we must live in light of the understanding that God is always with us. We are dwelling with God; we are beholding God; and we are talking with God. Constant worship is our way of life. God is a refuge to those who worship him.

Those who worship God will enjoy special privileges – he will protect them in times of trouble. The psalmist says,

> He shall hide me in His pavilion;
>> In the secret place of His tabernacle, He shall hide me;
>> He shall set me high upon a rock (Ps. 27.5).

The psalmist is trusting in God's ability to hide him from all danger. The worshiper will be hidden in God's 'pavilion', that is, his shelter. The worshiper will be protected in the secret place of the tabernacle. If that is not sufficient protection, he will be set high upon a rock. He would be placed upon a rock, because a high rock is a place of safety and a place of security. Remember the words of Ps. 40.2, 'he brought me up also out of a horrible pit, and he set my feet upon a rock, and established my going'. God is a refuge for those who worship him.

God is the Savior of Those Who Call upon His Name.
At this point in his experience, the psalmist is not facing any particular threat, but he prays that God will hear his cries for help should he ever find himself in trouble. Therefore, he entreats the Lord saying,

> ⁷ **Hear, O Lord, when I cry with my voice!**
>> **Have mercy also upon me, and answer me.**
> ⁸ **When You said, 'Seek My face,'**
>> **My heart said to You, 'Your face, Lord, I will seek.'**
> ⁹ **Do not hide Your face from me;**

> Do not turn Your servant away in anger;
> You have been my help;
> Do not leave me nor forsake me,
>   O God of my salvation.
> ¹⁰ When my father and my mother forsake me,
>   Then the LORD will take care of me (Ps. 27.7-10).

First, the psalmist implores God for continuing mercy. Second, he promises to respond whenever God summons him to prayer. That is, his heart is always ready to seek God. Third, he pleads for God's ongoing presence in his life. Fourth, he affirms the Lord's tender care. Even when his father and mother forsake him, the Lord will take him up. The Lord rescues those who call upon him.

When we are in trouble, we have several choices available to us. First, we can choose to trust in our own resources and abilities to extract ourselves from trouble. Second, we can choose to call on other people for help (a step that we should take more often in light of the Bible's exhortation that we confess our weaknesses one to another. We are encouraged to bear one another's burdens). However, we can also choose to take a third course of action – we can call upon the Lord.

The psalmist says, 'Hear, O Lord … do not hide your face'. Have you ever prayed when you felt like your prayers were not reaching God? Have you ever prayed when you did not feel like God was listening? When we pray, we may not feel like God is listening; but we must trust that he is. We must come to God with an urgency in our prayers. There comes a time when we must persist in prayer and persevere in prayer.

There comes a time when we must be strong in our prayers, like the Canaanite woman who was following after Jesus. She cried continually, 'Jesus, have mercy; my daughter is severely demon possessed' (Mt. 15.22-28). The disciples of Jesus commanded that she be quiet, because she was a Gentile woman. They said to her, 'Jesus came to minister to the Jews, not to the Gentiles'. Yet, Jesus asked her, 'What do you want?' She replied, 'I want my daughter to be healed.' Jesus rebuffed her request, saying that he did not come to feed the dogs (meaning Gentiles). However, she responded to the rejection with added faith. She said, 'Even the dogs eat the crumbs that fall from the master's table.' At that point, Jesus replied, 'I have not seen such faith in all of Israel. Go your way; your daughter is healed.' It is this kind of persistence that God wants to hear in our prayers; and when we cry out to him with passionate faith, he will hear us.

God is a Steadfast Guide for Those Who Rely on Him.
The psalmist maintains that even if his father and mother should forsake him, the Lord will continue to care for him. Furthermore, if his father and mother are not available to teach and guide him or fail to do so, he can depend upon the Lord to be his teacher and guide. The psalmist says,

> ¹¹ **Teach me Your way, O LORD,**
>   **And lead me in a smooth path,**
>   **because of my enemies.**
> ¹² **Do not deliver me to the will of my adversaries;**
>   **For false witnesses have risen against me,**
>   **And such as breathe out violence.**
> ¹³ **I would have lost heart, unless I had believed**
>   **That I would see the goodness of the LORD**
>   **In the land of the living.**
> ¹⁴ **Wait on the LORD; Be of good courage,**
>   **And He shall strengthen your heart;**
>   **Wait, I say, on the LORD! (Ps. 27.11-14)**

The psalmist trusts that God will be his guide. He prays, 'Teach me your way, O Lord'. God's ways are not our ways. We have our own ways. We have our own plans, and we have our own schemes and ideas. David, however, prays, 'Teach me *your* way, O Lord'.

Whenever we have choices to make, we may weigh the pros and cons of each option that is available to us. However, we do not know the future, and we do not have wisdom equal to the wisdom of God. We are not aware of all aspects of a problem, but God is!

We need to realize that when we trust in the Lord, he will lead us in the right way – his way, not our way. He will lead us in the way that he wants us to go. He knows what is best for us, and he knows the future. He knows the path that we need to take.

If we trust in him, God will lead us. However, God does not always answer us as quickly as we would like. The psalmist, therefore, encourages us to 'wait upon the Lord and be of good courage'. Waiting on the Lord is difficult for us, and we can grow quite impatient.

We want to know the answers, and we want to know them now. Waiting is not something we enjoy; but we need to come to the place where we can trust God and say, 'Lord, my life is in your hands. My future is in your hands; my way is in your hands. And Lord God, I will wait upon you, and I will trust in you.'

Psalm 27 teaches us to put our trust and faith in God. In the last verse, David tells us to 'wait on the Lord and be of good courage.' He means that we are to wait in faith, not in doubt. That is why he said, 'be of good courage.' We wait with confidence; we wait with hope; we wait with trust; and we wait with faith, not with fear.

When I was a boy, my mother told me an old story called 'Chicken Little'. An acorn fell from a tree and struck Chicken Little on the head. Greatly alarmed, Chicken Little ran from one person to another crying out, 'The sky is falling; the sky is falling'. We must not take on the attitude of Chicken Little while we are waiting on God. Any suspicions that the sky is falling are counterproductive to our faith and to our prayers. We wait upon God in full anticipation that he will hear our prayers and he will provide for us the guidance that we need. We may not know what God will do; but we know he will act, and he will act powerfully. He will do something. We would do well to remember the promise of Isa. 40.31, which says, 'They that wait upon the Lord shall renew their strength. They shall mount up with wings like an eagle. They shall run and not be weary; they shall walk and not faint'. Wait upon the Lord. The Lord is our light; the Lord is our salvation; and the Lord is the strength of our lives. When we are in trouble, when we are in need, and when we are in distress, we must wait upon the Lord and trust in him. He is our guide, and we can trust in him.

The Lord is watching over us. In Luke 12, Jesus said that God sees every sparrow that falls. How much more does God care for us than for the sparrows! Jesus explained that God sees every deed that we do and every thought that we think. God has numbered the hairs of our heads. God understands and knows exactly who we are, where we are, and where we need to be going with our lives. With David, we can say, 'Wait on the Lord and be of good courage, and he will strengthen your heart'.

Conclusion

We may want to offer a prayer like this:

> Oh Lord, I bow before you in humility, yet in confidence. My confidence rests in your grace and in your goodness. You have promised to be my guide, and I come to you now, asking for that guidance that only you can give. You are my teacher, and I confess that I need to learn from you. I need to trust in you and to rely upon you. Oh Lord, help me to stop doubting your love and resisting your grace. I praise you; I worship you; and I glorify you. Let me stand fast through the difficult times, and let my life be a witness to everyone who is around me. Oh Lord, you are my light; you are my salvation; and you are the strength of my life. I will not be afraid. When the enemy comes against me, he will stumble and fall. With your help, I will dwell in your house; and I will worship you. I will glorify you. Hallelujah!

Connecting with the Psalm

(Questions for discussion)

What does it mean to you that God is your 'light'?

What does it mean to you that God is the 'strength' of your life?

Have you ever felt surrounded by enemies? Read 2 Cor. 4.8-9 and compare Paul's experience to Psalm 27.

How does corporate worship add power to our prayers?

How does this psalm affect the way that you will pray from now on?

What if ... ?

(Creative and imaginative ideas)

What if we express our trust in God to a different friend or neighbor every day?

What if we prayerfully identify the areas of our lives where it is most difficult to trust God?

What if we make a list of reasons why we can trust God?

Now, come up with your own 'What if ... ?'

5

THE PASSIONATE PURSUIT OF A FAITHFUL TESTIMONY: PSALM 30

Setting the Direction

The Gospel of Luke tells the story of ten desperate lepers who sought out Jesus for his healing touch. As Jesus entered their village, they stood at a distance, afraid to approach him because their leprosy made them 'untouchable'.

> And they lifted up their voices and said, 'Jesus, Master, have mercy on us!' So when He saw them, He said to them, 'Go, show yourselves to the priests.' And so it was that as they went, they were cleansed. And one of them, when he saw that he was healed, returned, and with a loud voice glorified God, and fell down on his face at His feet, giving Him thanks. And he was a Samaritan. So Jesus answered and said, 'Were there not ten cleansed? But where are the nine? 'Were there not any found who returned to give glory to God except this foreigner?' And He said to him, 'Arise, go your way. Your faith has made you well.' (Lk. 17.12-19)

The story of the ten lepers illustrates the value of giving thanks to God. When God does something for us, we should thank him. When God hears our cries and does a mighty work in our lives, we must not simply go on our way. On the contrary, we must stop what we are doing and return to give thanks to God for his mercy and grace. All of the ten lepers were healed, but only one returned to give thanks. The other nine went on about their business. The one grateful leper praised and glorified God with a 'loud voice'. He was not ashamed for other people to hear what had happened. He did not go back and whisper it to Jesus, but he spoke it loudly. Like this leper who fell down at the feet of Jesus, we should be praising God with our voices at every opportunity. We can never praise God too much. Paul encouraged us saying, 'in everything give thanks, for this is the will of God in Christ Jesus concerning you' (1 Thess. 5.18 KJV). Like Paul, the psalmist teaches us the value of constant praise. At all times we should be giving thanks to God. Psalm 30 teaches us that we should worship God with our thankful testimony; that is, we should praise God with a testimony of what the Lord has done for us.

Discussion Starters

Why do we forget to praise God for his blessings?

What are the positive effects of gratitude to God?

Why have testimonies been virtually eliminated from our worship services?

Discuss the ways that God has been good to you.

Hearing the Word of God

Psalm 30

A Psalm. A Song at the dedication of the house of David.

1 I will extol You, O LORD, for You have lifted me up,
   And have not let my foes rejoice over me.
2 O LORD my God, I cried out to You,
   And You healed me.
3 O LORD, You brought my soul up from the grave;
   You have kept me alive,
   that I should not go down to the pit.
4 Sing praise to the LORD, You saints of His,
   And give thanks at the remembrance of
   His holy name.
5 For His anger is but for a moment,
   His favor is for life;
   Weeping may endure for a night,
   But joy comes in the morning.
6 Now in my prosperity I said,
   'I shall never be moved.'
7 LORD, by Your favor
   You have made my mountain stand strong;
   You hid Your face, and I was troubled.
8 I cried out to You, O LORD;
   And to the LORD I made supplication:
9 'What profit is there in my blood,
   When I go down to the pit? Will the dust praise You?
   Will it declare Your truth?
10 Hear, O LORD, and have mercy on me;
   LORD, be my helper!'
11 You have turned for me my mourning into dancing;
   You have put off my sackcloth
   and clothed me with gladness,
12 To the end that my glory may sing praise to You
   and not be silent.
   O LORD my God, I will give thanks to You forever.

Worship through Thankful Testimony

As we look at Psalm 30, there are at least two things that we should notice. First, we should notice how the Lord is addressed near the first of many of the verses. This Psalm is directed toward the Lord, and the psalmist puts the Lord up front in his praise. In our testimonies, God should claim priority. We may be tempted to praise ourselves as much or more than we praise God. Our praise should be directed to God. We should say, 'You healed me. You brought me up. You turned my mourning into dancing. You clothed me with joy. You kept me alive.' Our praise needs to be offered directly to God.

Suddenly in v. 4, however, after praising God directly, the psalmist changes direction and begins speaking to the people. He invites the congregation: 'Sing praise to the Lord.' He encourages them to praise God along with him. His invitation reminds me of another psalm where he sings, 'O magnify the Lord with me, and let us exalt his name together' (Ps. 34.3).

The Title of Psalm 30

A Psalm. A Song at the dedication of the house of David.

The title of this psalm is 'A Psalm. A Song at the dedication of the house of David'. The 'house of David' is the palace that he built near the end of his life. The psalm does not refer to the dedication of the temple, because David's son Solomon would build the temple after the death of David. David desired to build the temple, but God would not allow him to do so. David prayed and said, 'Lord, I have built a beautiful new house, and now I would like to build a house for you.' Sadly, the Lord replied, 'it is not for you to build my house, because you have been a man of war; your son will build my house'. And then God added, 'but I will build your house' (2 Sam. 7.27). The word 'house' refers to David's household, his royal dynasty. God goes on to say that a son of David will always be upon the throne of Israel.

The Psalmist's Praise

> ¹ I will extol You, O LORD, for You have lifted me up,
>   And have not let my foes rejoice over me.
> ² O LORD my God, I cried out to You,
>   And You healed me.
> ³ O LORD, You brought my soul up from the grave;
>   You have kept me alive,
>   that I should not go down to the pit (Ps. 30.1-3).

Psalm 30 starts out with the words, 'I will extol you, O LORD'. The word 'extol' means to raise up high; therefore, in the context of worship, extol means to exalt, magnify, to lift up God's name. Why should we extol God? We lift him up because he has lifted us up. The Hebrew word that is translated 'lifted up' means to pull up, such as pulling up of a water bucket out of the well. Therefore, we exalt him because he has reached down and pulled us up. It reminds me of Psalm 40 where David said, 'he pulled me up out of a horrible pit, out of the miry clay, and he set my feet upon a rock' (v. 2). We were in the pit, but he lifted us up; and because he lifted us up, we will raise him up. We will lift him up in praise. Here in Psalm 30, David praises God for keeping him free of the pit: 'you preserved my life that I should not go down into the pit' (v. 3).

David also praises God for hearing his pleas when he had cried out to God and for healing him. The word 'cried' is not the usual Hebrew expression for calling upon God. There are two words that are used commonly in the Old Testament. The word *qara* means to cry out in the sense of making noise, an audible utterance. It is also used of reading aloud such as reading a letter, and it is used of greeting someone, calling out, 'Hello'. Another word that means to cry out is *tsaʿaq*, which signifies calling out for help. The word used in Ps. 30.2 is neither of those; instead, the word used here means to scream over and over, to cry out loudly and continually. David is saying, 'Oh Lord, I was screaming out for help to you, and you healed me'.

Then, the psalmist expands his reason for praise. He says, 'You brought up my soul from the grave, you kept me alive that I should not go down into the pit'. It says literally, 'you preserved my life from the pit'. Our lives are in the hands of God; he preserves us from death. Therefore, let us praise him.

The Congregation's Praise

> [4] **Sing praise to the LORD, You saints of His,**
>   **And give thanks at the remembrance of**
>   **His holy name.**
> [5] **For His anger is but for a moment,**
>   **His favor is for life;**
>   **Weeping may endure for a night,**
>   **But joy comes in the morning (Ps. 30.4-5).**

Next, the psalmist speaks to the congregation, summoning them to join him in worship. He invites them, 'Sing praise to the Lord'. The Hebrew word 'sing' refers to playing a musical instrument, to plucking the strings. A better translation would be, 'make music unto the Lord'. The Lord loves music. He never tires of listening to our music when it is offered in praise to him. Pentecostals have always been known for their music, and we should continue to be known for our music. Our churches should be filled with the music of praise: the sound of the piano, the keyboard, the organ, the trumpet, the drums, the guitar, and every other kind of instrument. God loves music. Make music to the Lord!

He says, 'make music to the Lord, you saints'. The word 'saints' here is also unusual. The common word for saint is *qadosh*, which means holy one. But the word used here is *hasid*, meaning faithful one. *Hasid* comes from the Hebrew word *hesed*, which signifies covenant faithfulness. In fact, one conservative Jewish group known as the Hasidim (or Hasidic Jews) derive their name from *hasid*, to signify their faithfulness to the Torah. The psalmist, therefore, is inviting everyone who is faithful to the covenant to praise God. He is saying, 'Everyone who is faithful, come and praise God. Make music to the Lord, faithful people'. God's faithful followers should sing praise, make music, and give thanks. Giving thanks signifies testifying publicly, giving a praise testimony.

This worship in music and praise should take place 'at the remembrance of His holy name'. Whenever we remember that God is holy, we should praise him. What does it mean when we say that God is holy? It means that God always acts in accordance with his character of justice and love. That is, God's nature is consistent. He is a God of integrity. His nature is righteous, good, and just. Everything that God does flows out of his love and righteousness.

God does get angry, but he never gets angry without good reason; and his anger is always momentary. The Hebrew says literally, 'his anger is a moment'. His anger is always justified, and it is manifested only in redemptive ways. It is intended to produce human change for the good.

God's anger is momentary, but 'his favor is for life' (v. 5). The King James Version uses the word 'favor', but a better translation is 'pleasure'. Therefore, the psalmist is saying that God is only angry with us for a moment, but he takes pleasure in us as long as we live. God takes pleasure in his people forever. He looks upon us with great pleasure, and that is a wonderful thing. It is very much the way that we look upon our children – with joy. When we think of our children, it brings great pleasure to our hearts. We are well aware that our children will do things that we do not approve of, and they will at times disappoint us. Sometimes, we are even angry at our children, but our anger is temporary. Our pleasure in them lasts all the days of their lives.

God's anger does not last and neither does our sorrow – 'Weeping may endure for a night, but joy comes in the morning'. The words, 'endure for a night', mean literally to take lodging overnight. That is, weeping is only a temporary guest, like a guest in a motel who stays only for the night. Weeping will come in and take the spare bed and stay for the night, but joy (literally 'the shout') will come in the morning. Even if we sleep with weeping, we can wake up with shouting. The psalm is teaching us the temporary nature of sorrow and pain. God's people certainly face troubles, but troubles do not last. However, the joy of the Lord lasts forever. Many afflictions come to righteous people, but 'the Lord delivers them from them all' (Ps. 34.8). When we are going through a time of trouble, we think the pain will never end; but it will. One night of suffering can seem like an eternity, but joy comes in the morning.

The Psalmist's Testimony

⁶ Now in my prosperity I said,
  'I shall never be moved.'
⁷ LORD, by Your favor
  You have made my mountain stand strong;

You hid Your face, and I was troubled.
⁸ I cried out to You, O LORD;
And to the LORD I made supplication:
⁹ 'What profit is there in my blood,
When I go down to the pit? Will the dust praise You?
Will it declare Your truth?
¹⁰ Hear, O LORD, and have mercy on me;
LORD, be my helper!'
¹¹ You have turned for me my mourning into dancing;
You have put off my sackcloth
and clothed me with gladness,
¹² To the end that my glory may sing praise to You
and not be silent.
O Lord my God,
I will give thanks to You forever (Ps. 30.6-12).

His Previous Time of Distress

Next, the psalmist goes back and recounts his trouble. He says, 'in my prosperity (a time of quietness or ease, when everything was going well), I said, 'I will never be moved' (shaken). He believed that his prosperity would continue and that he would never be shaken. However, he was mistaken; therefore, he says, 'Lord, … you hid your face, and I was troubled' (disturbed).

His Previous Cry for Help

He says, 'I cried out to you, Lord'. The word 'cried' is *tsa'aq*, the usual word for crying out for help. In addition to crying out, he 'made supplication'. Supplication means to seek for God's favor, to seek for God's grace. David was in need, and he cried out to the Lord, and he gives the content of his prayer. He tells us exactly what he prayed. In his prayer, he asked, 'What profit (gain) is there in my blood, when I go down to the pit? Will the dust praise you? Will it declare your truth?' (v. 9) David is asking if the dust of his decayed body will offer testimony to God's goodness. He reasons that if he dies, his testimony will be silenced. He also pleads with God, 'Hear, O Lord and have mercy (show favor, grace) on me. Lord, be my helper.' He prays for God's mercy, grace, and help.

His Previous Deliverance

God answered David's prayer. The answer is stated here in figurative terms. The psalmist shouts, 'You have turned my mourning into dancing' (v. 11). Here is the answer. The word 'mourning' means literally 'wailing'. God answered and turned his wailing into dancing. It was common in biblical times for mourners to wail and scream out in anguish. They would even hire mourners at times in order to make a greater impact. For David, however, the mourning garments of sackcloth have been replaced with 'gladness'. Joy has returned to his house.

His Promise to Continue Praising God

The psalmist declares that God's act of deliverance has a purpose. God answered his prayers so that he might 'sing praise' to God, make music to the Lord, and 'not be silent' (v. 12). In one final burst of gratitude, he proclaims, 'O Lord my God, I will give thanks to you forever'. The word 'thanks' is *yadah*, which means the offering of a thankful testimony of praise for this specific divine intervention. Psalm 30, therefore, begins with praise – 'I will extol you Lord' – and ends with praise – 'I will continue to praise you'. We can never praise God too much. Let us begin our days with praise and end our days with praise. Let us praise him! God is listening. Let us pray in times of need, and let us praise him when he answers. God is interested in our lives; he is interested in what is happening. We cannot see him, but he is here. We know this by faith. If we listen to the voices around us in the world, we conclude that God does not exist or does not care. Instead, we should listen to Jesus, who said, 'I will never leave you and I will never forsake you' (Heb. 13.5). Therefore, let us pray, and let us praise.

Songs of Praise

There are two kinds of praise psalms in the book of Psalms. One type of praise psalm, exemplified by Psalm 30, is a psalm that praises God for a specific act that God has done. We call this a psalm of thankful testimony. The second type of praise psalm is called the hymn. The hymn praises God not for one specific answer to prayer or deliverance but for God's nature and character. We will take a look at the hymns in a later chapter.

The psalm of thankful testimony, sometimes called the thanksgiving psalm, records the praises of an individual who has received an answer to prayer. This person returns to God and says, 'Lord, I was in trouble and you helped me; I was lost and you found me; I was in need and you supplied that need. You delivered me; you came to my rescue; and now I want to praise you for your answer, for your help, for your deliverance'. Again, a psalm of thankful testimony is a praise psalm that gives thanks to God for a specific action in the life of an individual or in the congregation.

Genuine Praise and Deep Prayer

The psalms of thankful praise are related to the psalms of urgent prayer that we studied earlier. More specifically, the relationship between prayer psalms and praise psalms shows that praise is a product of prayer. Psalms 13 and 22 are both prayers that were uttered by the psalmist in the midst of trouble, from the pit of despair. In these prayers, the psalmist brings his need before God. He prays, 'How long, O LORD, will you forget me?' (Ps. 13.1) He cries out, 'My God, my God, why have you forsaken me?' (Ps. 22.1) In the prayer psalms, the psalmist describes an urgent need and calls upon God's assistance. The painful experience of the psalmist is expressed in the form of a petition to God. In one case he prays, 'O LORD my God, save me' (Ps. 7.1). Within that same psalm, there is a promise of praise. The psalmist says, 'I will praise the LORD according to his righteousness, and I will sing praise to the name of the LORD most high' (Ps. 7.17). The psalmist promises that whenever God answers, he will praise God.

That promise of praise is very important. What God wants from us more than anything else is our love and devotion. If he has our heart, then he has all of us. Jesus said, 'you shall love the Lord your God with all your heart'; this is the greatest commandment (Mt. 22.37-38). As Christians, it is our desire to live a life that pleases God. Thus, we try to do things that will please God. However, in all of our activity, let us not forget to express our praise, thanksgiving, and affection for God. As we walk in relationship with God, we must remember that God appreciates a grateful heart. He appreciates our worship of him and the giving of ourselves to him as a living sacrifice (Rom. 12.1).

Prayer that Precedes Praise

So, first comes the prayer –

'How long, O Lord' (Ps. 13.1).

Then comes the praise –

'I will sing unto the Lord' (Ps. 13.6).

Likewise, Psalm 22 begins with prayer –

'My God, my God, why have you forsaken me?' (v. 1)

Afterwards, comes a promise of praise –

'My praise shall be of you in the great assembly' (v. 25).

Notice the future tense used by the psalmist: 'I will praise you'; 'I will give you thanks'; and 'I will sing praises'.

The Vow of Praise

Finally, near the end of Psalm 22, he declares, 'I will pay my vows'. The vow is a promise to offer up a sacrifice in the temple called a thanksgiving offering. So, the psalms of prayer include a promise to praise God. The psalmist declares, 'my praise shall be of you in the great assembly. I will pay my vows for those who fear him' (v. 25). The recital of the psalm of thanksgiving is a part of the psalmist's fulfillment of his promise to praise God. The person who prays the urgent prayer of lament puts it in the form of a psalm, and that psalm includes a promise to praise God once the prayer is answered. When the answer comes, the person who prayed will compose a psalm of praise in fulfillment of their promise. Therefore, the psalm of urgent prayer is followed by the psalm of thankful testimony.

Praise and thanksgiving issues forth from the heart of prayer. Praise is shallow and empty if it does not come forth from a prayerful life. In order to praise God fully, we must first spend time in the presence of God, prayerfully submitting ourselves to God and seeking the face of God. We must first surrender to God, bring our needs before God, and turn them over to God. We cannot ignore God throughout the week and then walk into God's house on Sunday with the expectation that he will pour out his Spirit upon us and bless our praises. Without prayer, our praises are shallow and empty. Deep and heartfelt prayer always precedes Pentecost. Glorious times of praise and worship are always built upon the foundation of prayer and fasting. We must open ourselves up and pour ourselves out to God before he will pour out his Spirit upon us. The greatest praise comes after we have taken time to seek God with all our hearts. When we have sought God diligently and urgently and when God has answered our prayers and delivered us from the enemy, then praise will come easily from our lips. No one will have to beg us to worship. The pastor will not have to prompt us to praise God. The worship leader will find it easy to lead, because we will be ready to praise God.

The Thanksgiving Sacrifice

The psalm of thanksgiving is the fulfillment of the promise to praise God. Further, the vow refers to a thanksgiving offering. The person whose prayer God had answered would bring a sacrifice to the temple as a sacrifice of praise. This thanksgiving sacrifice would vary according to the financial abilities of the giver. The animal would be brought to the temple and handed over to the priest, who would slaughter the animal. The skin of the animal, along with its insides, would be burned on the altar. The edible parts of the animal, the meat, would be cooked in a pot of boiling water. Once the meat had finished cooking, the priest would take a large fork and stick it down into the meat. Whatever portion was retrieved with the fork belonged to the priest. The remainder of the cooked meat would form the basis of a fellowship meal for the person who made the sacrifice and for his family and friends. During this fellowship meal, which we could also call a thanksgiving meal, the person who offered the sacrifice would share a testimony of God's gracious work in his or her life. They would tell the story of their time of trouble, their prayer, and God's deliverance. Everyone would celebrate what God had done in the life of the believer, and they would sing songs of testimony and praise. According to Lev. 7.16, a sacrifice offered in fulfillment of a vow should be eaten on the same day that the sacrifice was made. The worshipers should eat the sacrifice either at or near the temple in celebration of the testimony of the person who had been delivered by the power of God.

The testimony was given publicly to the family, friends, and the congregation that had gathered. We often overlook the fact that in the Bible, the word 'thanksgiving' does not refer to a private attitude of gratefulness. The giving of thanks is not a private matter; it is a public display of testimony and witness to God's work. It is a public, outward testimony to the congregation of what God has done. The biblical concept of thanksgiving always involves public testimony of praise.

Outline of the Psalms of Thanksgiving

These thanksgiving psalms, although they vary in form, will normally have three parts. First is the introduction; second is a narration of the divine intervention; and third is the conclusion. In the introduction, the psalmist will declare his or her intention to praise the Lord: 'I will praise the Lord'. The psalmist will then give a general reason for praising the Lord. The second part of the psalm, the narration, looks back and recounts the events of being in trouble, the prayer to God, and God's answer. The third part of the psalm, the conclusion, restates the psalmist's intent to praise God; and it will offer descriptive praise to God. Descriptive praise is praise for God's character and nature, a statement of God's goodness. For example the statement, 'The Lord is great and greatly to be praised', is descriptive praise. Descriptive praise does not mention a specific event; instead, it declares God's positive attributes.

We can outline the psalms of thanksgiving as follows (references to Psalm 30 are in parentheses).

I. Introduction
   A. Intent to Praise God (v. 1a)
   B. Summary of Why (v. 1b-3)
II. Narration of the Divine Intervention
   A. Distress (vv. 6-7)
   B. Cry for Help (vv. 8-10)
   C. Deliverance (v. 11)
III. Conclusion
   A. Renewed Vow of Praise (v. 12)
   B. Descriptive Praise (vv. 4-5)

Let us apply this structure to Psalm 30. The psalmist starts out with the intent to praise God: 'I will extol you Lord'. This is the beginning of the psalm. Then he gives a reason for praise: 'because you have lifted me up, and you have not let my enemies rejoice over me. Oh LORD, I cried to you for help and you healed me.' Next comes the narration, in which the psalmist tells in more detail what happened. This second part of the thanksgiving psalm tells about the specific events surrounding the psalmist's need, the prayer, and God's answer. David relates his situation by saying, 'In my prosperity I said, "I will never be moved", and you hid your face from me, and I was dismayed'. His trouble is summarized in terms of God's absence, which resulted in the psalmist's feelings of dismay. Next, he relates that he sought God in prayer: 'but to you O LORD, I cried, and I made supplication'. He looks back to his time of prayer and restates the words that he uttered to God. Next, he tells about his deliverance. 'I was in trouble; I cried out; but you have turned my mourning into dancing'.

The truth is that many Christians practice neither prevailing prayer nor passionate praise. It is not that we lack occasions for urgent prayer. We all have occasions of great need, times of suffering, times of pain, times of grief, and times of sorrow. However, when we encounter pressure, pain, and suffering, we are tempted to pursue one of two unhelpful options. First, we may give up, resigning ourselves to a life of suffering. If we do not believe that God is genuinely involved in our lives and that he will intervene, then prayer is essentially a ritual that accomplishes little. Do we really believe that God answers prayer? The second unhelpful option is the positive confession approach. We could also call this the 'denial of reality' approach. Some well-meaning faith teachers have told us that we should never speak any negative words. We should never confess that we are weak, that we are sick, that we have doubts, or that we are struggling in any way. They say that we should only speak words of victory, conquest, prosperity, health, wealth, joy, rejoicing, and happiness. Such an approach, however, is not biblical. Instead of denying that we are weak, the Bible teaches us to admit our weaknesses. Instead of denying that we are sick, the Bible tells us to call upon other believers to pray for us that we may be healed. As we mentioned earlier, the psalms of urgent prayer, in which sin is confessed and pain is expressed, are the most common type of psalm in the book of Psalms.

It also is not the case that we lack occasions to utter exuberant praise. The many times that God intervenes in our lives are just such occasions. He answers our prayers, so let us praise him. He heals our sicknesses, so let us praise him. He blesses our children, so let us praise him. He delivers us from danger, so let us praise him. In our culture, exuberant and passionate emotion is commonly limited to the rock concert and the sports stadium. If we can be enthusiastic about the transitory and ultimately insignificant results of a sports contest, then why can we not become enthusiastic in our worship of the God of the universe, creator of all things, the sustainer of life, the King of kings, and the Lord of lords who is coming to rule and reign over the earth in his eternal kingdom?

In times of pain, we ought to be praying; and in times of joy, we ought to be shouting. The psalmist says, 'he has replaced my sack-cloth with gladness' (30.11). What is sackcloth? It is the cheap and rough cloth that was worn in ancient times as a sign of mourning. Its significance is similar to the more recent practice of wearing black. The removal of sackcloth is a symbolic way of saying to God, 'you have removed my grief'. The Psalms are written in poetic form; and they use figurative, vivid language to go beyond the simple statement of deliverance. Mourning is turned into dancing, and sackcloth is turned into gladness. The language is moving and exciting.

The psalm ends with a renewed vow of praise: 'Oh LORD God, I will give thanks to you forever'. In many cases, the psalms of thanks-giving conclude with a verse of descriptive praise. In Psalm 30, how-ever, the descriptive praise is in the middle of the psalm. The writers of the psalms had the liberty of moving things around within the structures of the psalm types. The outlines of the psalm types were not static but were dynamic. The descriptive praise is found in vv. 4-5: 'Sing praise to the LORD, you his saints; give thanks to his holy name, for his anger is momentary, but his favor is lifelong'. David is calling on the congregation to give praise along with him. He exhorts the believers to praise God in response to God's nature and character. The specific attribute that the psalmist points to is God's grace, his favor. The anger of God is temporary, but the grace of God is for-ever. Humans sometimes provoke God's anger, but his anger does not last. Anger is not a part of the nature of God; rather, it is a re-sponse to human sin and disobedience. The anger of God only lasts for a short time; but his grace, his favor, endures throughout our lives. His favor never expires; it never runs out; it is never depleted; and it is never insufficient.

Conclusion

The song of testimony, or thanksgiving psalm, is a public celebration of answered prayer. It is a public testimonial to all who are present that God has intervened in the life of the worshiper. The thanksgiving psalm is based upon the final element of the lament. At the end of the lament, the petitioner promises that when the prayer has been answered, he or she will offer a thanksgiving sacrifice. After God has answered the prayer and brought deliverance, the psalmist comes with his or her family and friends to the temple. At the temple, an offering or sacrifice is made in thanks to God. The worshipers enjoy a meal together, and a song of testimony is sung to commemorate the occasion in praise to God.

The song of testimony teaches us the value of public thanksgiving. This kind of psalm is meant to encourage the congregation who hear the song. Our deliverance is not complete until we give witness to the answer. God's purposes in bringing deliverance are incomplete without our testimony. The song of testimony teaches us the value of sharing our personal experiences with others. Our children need to hear that God has answered our prayers. Our friends and family need to hear what God has done in our lives. Some churches have become very impersonal, and the members of the congregation no longer share their lives with each other. These psalms demonstrate the value of telling our story to one another in the context of worship.

The songs of testimony include Psalms 30, 34, 41, 66, 84, 87, 91, 92, 103, 111, 116, 118, 121, 122, 131, 138, 139, and 146.

Connecting with the Psalm

(Questions for discussion)

Can you name a specific prayer that God answered for you, for a loved one, or for a friend?

What are the benefits of gratitude?

How does our testimony help to form our children and grandchildren in the faith?

How can we better celebrate the victories that God gives us?

Explain how sincere prayer leads to powerful praise.

What if ... ?

(Creative and imaginative ideas)

What if we share on social media a specific testimony of answered prayer?

What if we find ways to include more testimonies in our worship services and group meetings?

What if we start recording our testimonies on video for the benefit of our children and grandchildren?

What if we ask other believers to share their testimonies with us so that we can rejoice with them?

Now, come up with your own 'What if ... ?'

6

THE PASSIONATE PURSUIT OF PURITY: PSALM 51

Setting the Direction

One goal of this study is that we become better worshipers as we passionately pursue God. People have different ideas about the nature of worship. Some people believe that worship consists entirely of singing and praising God, but the Psalms teach us that prayer is also an important part of worship. Jesus recognized the necessity of prayer; and he declared, 'my house shall be called a house of prayer' (Mt. 21.13, quoting Isa. 56.7). The Apostle Paul, instructing young pastor Timothy about proper worship, writes, 'Therefore I exhort first of all that supplications, prayers, intercessions, and giving of thanks be made for all' people (1 Tim. 2.1).

Not only must prayer be a vital *component* of every worship service, prayer must also be a part of our *preparation* for worship. Through his prayer of confession in Psalm 51, David prepares his heart to reenter the presence of God. The pursuit of God includes the pursuit of purity. In the Old Testament, the priests were required to wear clean white robes and to wash their hands before entering the temple. Sacrifices were offered that cleansed the temple and that represented a cleansing of people's sins. The purity of heart that is required of worshipers is emphasized in Psalm 24, which says, 'Who may go up unto the hill of the LORD? Who may stand in his holy place? He who has clean hands and a pure heart, who has not lifted up his soul unto vanity nor sworn deceitfully. He shall receive blessing from the LORD'

(vv. 3-4). Before we proceed to worship God, we should examine our hearts and pray for cleansing and purification.

Jesus spoke a parable to those who saw no need to seek for purity of heart. He said,

> Two men went up to the temple to pray, one a Pharisee and the other a tax collector. The Pharisee stood and prayed thus with himself, 'God, I thank You that I am not like other men – extortioners, unjust, adulterers, or even as this tax collector. I fast twice a week; I give tithes of all that I possess.' And the tax collector, standing afar off, would not so much as raise his eyes to heaven, but beat his breast, saying, 'God, be merciful to me a sinner!' I tell you, this man went down to his house justified rather than the other; for everyone who exalts himself will be humbled, and he who humbles himself will be exalted (Lk. 18.10-14).

Confession of sin is not easy for some Pentecostal believers. We have taught rightly that Christians should be sanctified and live in victory over the power of sin. However, the emphasis on victorious living has made us hesitant to admit our failings. We do not want to admit that we have sinned. We have been taught that whoever is born of God does not continue to commit sin (1 Jn 3.9). Therefore, sin cannot be habitual behavior for the Christian. However, we also read that anyone who claims to have no sin is deceived (1 Jn 1.8). The good news for all of us is that if we sin, 'we have an advocate with the Father, Jesus Christ the righteous' (1 Jn 2.1); and if we 'confess our sins, he is faithful and just to forgive us our sins, and to cleanse us from all unrighteousness' (1 Jn 1.9). Our spiritual grandfather John Wesley taught that sanctified Christians do not willingly and actively pursue sin. Nevertheless, he insisted that because of our weaknesses, everyone commits unwitting sin every day. So he taught his followers to pray for daily cleansing and for daily forgiveness of sins.

I would suggest that the first thing that we do when we enter the presence of God is to ask him to search our hearts for anything that is unpleasing to him. As we come into worship, we should ask the Lord to cleanse us – to cleanse our hearts so that we may worship him without any barrier between us. In Psalm 139, David prays, 'Search me, O God, and know my heart: try me, and know my thoughts: And see if there be any wicked way in me, and lead me in the way everlasting' (vv. 23-24). As we come into worship, let us pray that nothing in our lives will be withheld from God, so that we may worship freely and openly with liberty in the Spirit. Let us pray that there be no hindrance in our lives, no selfishness, no deceitfulness, no guile, and that our hearts will be open completely to God. Prayers of repentance are essential for a Christian. To pray and ask God's forgiveness is necessary.

Discussion Starters

How often do you pray for purity of heart and life?

Is purity an important matter for you? Why? or Why not?

In your view, what is the root cause (or causes) of sinful behavior?

Is it necessary that Christians confess their sins?

Hearing the Word of God

Psalm 51

> To the Chief Musician. A Psalm of David when Nathan the prophet went to him, after he had gone in to Bathsheba.
> [1] Have mercy upon me, O God,
>   According to Your lovingkindness;
>   According to the multitude of Your tender mercies,
>   Blot out my transgressions.
> [2] Wash me thoroughly from my iniquity,
>   And cleanse me from my sin.
> [3] For I acknowledge my transgressions,
>   And my sin is always before me.
> [4] Against You, You only, have I sinned,
>   And done this evil in Your sight –
>   That You may be found just when You speak,
>   And blameless when You judge.
> [5] Behold, I was brought forth in iniquity,
>   And in sin my mother conceived me.
> [6] Behold, You desire truth in the inward parts,
>   And in the hidden part You will make me to
>   know wisdom.
> [7] Purge me with hyssop, and I shall be clean;
>   Wash me, and I shall be whiter than snow.
> [8] Make me hear joy and gladness,
>   That the bones You have broken may rejoice.
> [9] Hide Your face from my sins,
>   And blot out all my iniquities.
> [10] Create in me a clean heart, O God,
>   And renew a steadfast spirit within me.
> [11] Do not cast me away from Your presence,
>   And do not take Your Holy Spirit from me.
> [12] Restore to me the joy of Your salvation,
>   And uphold me by Your generous Spirit.
> [13] Then I will teach transgressors Your ways,
>   And sinners shall be converted to You.
> [14] Deliver me from the guilt of bloodshed, O God,
>   The God of my salvation,

And my tongue shall sing aloud of Your righteousness.
¹⁵ O Lord, open my lips,
And my mouth shall show forth Your praise.
¹⁶ For You do not desire sacrifice, or else I would give it;
You do not delight in burnt offering.
¹⁷ The sacrifices of God are a broken spirit,
A broken and a contrite heart –
These, O God, You will not despise.
¹⁸ Do good in Your good pleasure to Zion;
Build the walls of Jerusalem.
¹⁹ Then You shall be pleased with the sacrifices of
righteousness,
With burnt offering and whole burnt offering;
Then they shall offer bulls on Your altar.

A Psalm of Repentance

To the Chief Musician. A Psalm of David when Nathan the prophet went to him, after he had gone in to Bathsheba.

Psalm 51 is a personal prayer of repentance, what we might call a penitential psalm or a penitential lament. The heading situates this prayer in the life of David as a repentant response to the prophet Nathan's rebuke (2 Sam. 12.1-14). The psalm has been used by Jews and Christians for hundreds of years as a model for repentance. Whenever we need to pray a prayer of deep repentance and ask for God's forgiveness, we can use this psalm as a way of approaching God in prayer. It is an example of how we, as God's people, can come to the Lord for forgiveness, cleansing, and restoration when we have stumbled and fallen.

A Plea for Mercy

¹ Have mercy upon me, O God,
According to Your lovingkindness;
According to the multitude of Your tender mercies,
Blot out my transgressions.
² Wash me thoroughly from my iniquity,
And cleanse me from my sin (Ps. 51.1-2).

David does not mince words. He gets right to the point, 'Have mercy upon me, O God'. In Hebrew, the very first word of Psalm 51 is 'grace' – used in the form of a verb. The English language does not have a verb that signifies the giving of grace, but the Hebrew word here is a verb. Thus, David's prayer might be translated literally, 'Grace me, O God'; 'Favor me, O God'; 'Be gracious to me, O God'; or 'Show me grace, O God'.

This is a powerful way to begin the psalm. David does not waste words making futile excuses. We are tempted to minimize our sin and to offer one excuse or another, such as, 'I was trying', or 'I did my best', or 'I will do better next time'. When seeking God's forgiveness, all excuses are prideful and pointless. Our human efforts will never be sufficient; rather, we must learn to rest in the grace of God. We must throw ourselves at the foot of the cross, and cry out to God, 'Have mercy upon me a sinner'. We need God's grace. There is no other hope except grace.

Moreover, David does not compare his righteousness with that of others. The basis of his plea is not 'Be gracious to me, Lord, because I am a better man than my neighbor'. Instead, he prays pointedly, 'O God, give me grace'. In our pleas for pardon we must not argue that we are improving or making progress, and we must not exalt ourselves above others. No, we must plead for grace. There is no other way to forgiveness. There is no other hope for healing. Forgiveness and freedom come by grace alone.

David does not make excuses for his sin, and neither does he base his prayer upon his rank, position, status, or title. The basis of his plea is not 'God, give me grace because I am the king of Israel'. He does not argue, 'God, give me grace because I found myself in a bad situation'. Instead, his request for God's grace is based upon God's 'lovingkindness' and 'mercy'. Therefore, the basis of grace and forgiveness is the nature of God. God's nature is love, and it is God's nature to be gracious, merciful, and compassionate. As we stated in an earlier chapter, the Hebrew word for 'lovingkindness' (*ḥesed*) signifies covenant love or covenant faithfulness. God's covenant with us is at the very heart of his nature.

By using the word *ḥesed*, 'covenant faithfulness', David demonstrates that he considers himself to be already in a covenant relationship to God. That is, he is one of God's people, so his is not the prayer of an unbeliever. It is very important that we understand that David's repentance is not of someone who has been outside the church, outside the body of Christ, outside of the congregation of believers. David is a believer. He is one of God's people. He is a part of the congregation, but he has done wrong. As a believer, he says, 'God, have mercy upon me according to your covenant faithfulness'.

The focus here is not upon David's faithfulness but upon God's faithfulness. We do not come to God in worship based upon *our* faithfulness; we come to God in worship trusting in *God's* faithfulness. And again, we must realize that our salvation – the ground of our forgiveness, the ground of our pardon – is not our promise to do better. Of course, we *should* promise to do better. True repentance assumes a transformation of heart and a change of direction that leads to better behavior. Nevertheless, grace is not given on the basis of our self-improvement. Grace is given out of God's love to us.

Using different words, David repeats his request: 'According to the multitude of Your tender mercies, blot out my transgressions'. The words 'tender mercies' might also be translated 'affectionate compassion'. David's petition is based upon God's compassion, affection, and love as the ground of forgiveness.

Furthermore, he says, 'blot out my transgressions' – 'According to your affection for me, according to your compassion, wipe out the record of my evil choices'. It is as if his sins were written down and as if God could wipe them out and erase them as from a tablet. 'Erase my sins', he pleads. David repeats his request for forgiveness using two other parallel terms: 'wash' and 'cleanse'. He prays, 'Wash me thoroughly from my iniquity. Cleanse me from my sin'.

In addition to his use of three words to signify forgiveness (erase, wash, cleanse), he also uses three different words for wrongdoing, just to make it clear that he knows what he has done. First, he uses the word 'transgression' (Heb. *pesha*), which means a breaking of God's law, disobedience to God's commandments. Second, he uses the word 'iniquity' (Heb. *'avon*), which means a twisting or distorting of what is right. Some scholars think that it refers to waywardness or corruption. Third, he uses the word 'sin' (Heb. *hatah*), which is a deviation from God's commandments. These multiple terms display the multifaceted nature of sin. Is sin a rebellion against God? Yes. Is it a distortion of what is right? Yes. Is sin a deviation from God's commandments? Yes. Sin is all of these things and more, which is why the Old Testament includes so many different terms that specify the different aspects of sin – transgression, iniquity, sin. These terms refer to what happens when a person departs from God's will and from God's commandments. David confesses that he is guilty of every aspect of sin. He recognizes the magnitude of his guilt; therefore, he presents four requests to God: (1) 'Be gracious to me'. (2) 'Blot out my transgressions'. (3) 'Wash me from my iniquity'. (4) 'Cleanse me from my sin'. David knows the depth of his failure; he sees the urgency of his plight; and he desperately wants to be thoroughly and completely cleansed and purified.

The Pain and Depth of Sin

> ³ **For I acknowledge my transgressions,**
>   **And my sin is always before me.**
> ⁴ **Against You, You only, have I sinned,**
>   **And done this evil in Your sight –**
>   **That You may be found just when You speak,**
>   **And blameless when You judge.**
> ⁵ **Behold, I was brought forth in iniquity,**
>   **And in sin my mother conceived me.**
> ⁶ **Behold, You desire truth in the inward parts,**
>   **And in the hidden part**
>   **You will make me to know wisdom (Ps. 51.3-6).**

David says literally, 'I know my transgressions'. That is, he is constantly reminded of his disobedience and his failure. His sin is ever on his mind. Furthermore, he admits to God, 'Against you, you only have I sinned, and done this evil in your sight'. In his admission he adds a fourth word for sin: 'evil' (Heb. *ra*'). David's actions were 'evil' in the sight of God. The Hebrew word 'evil' suggests that David's disobedience produced harmful consequences – to himself, to his relationship with God, and to other people besides himself. He hurt other people.

David insists that his sin is ultimately against God alone. It is clear from Scripture that when we sin, we hurt other people and that we can sin against people. Therefore, David does not intend to say that his actions did not hurt other people. He is saying essentially that he cannot bring back from the dead Uriah the Hittite, whom he murdered; and his adultery cannot be undone. All he can do is ask God, whom he has offended, to restore the broken relationship between himself and God. Once we have sinned, we cannot undo it; but we can ask God for a restoration of fellowship.

David adds, 'that you may be just when you speak and blameless when you judge' (v. 4). Paul cites this verse as a way of explaining that our sin proves that God is righteous in his judgment of us (Rom. 3.4). None of us is righteous because 'all have sinned and come short of the glory of God' (Rom. 3.23). When God judges us, therefore, he is just; he is righteous in his judgment. We are guilty; but thankfully, Paul can add the assurance that 'where sin abounded, grace did much more unbound' (Rom. 5.20).

The psalmist continues to deepen his confession, stating, 'I was brought forth in iniquity, and in sin my mother conceived me'. He recognizes that his sin problem consists of more than one action, more than one weakness. In fact, his entire life is permeated by the influence of sin. Even before he was born, sinfulness was a part of him, residing in his nature. This is what theologians call original sin or the sin nature. As soon as children can begin to make choices, they will make a wrong choice. As soon as they have the capability to obey or disobey, they will choose to disobey. As soon as they have the ability to move, they will move in the wrong direction. As soon as they have the ability to speak, they will tell a lie. Sin is pervasive in the fallen human nature, and sin is serious. David admits that his problem is more than the commission of one sin and that his whole life has been influenced by sin. He needs constantly to come to God for cleansing, for purging, for help. He needs God's grace; he needs God's mercy.

A Plea for Thorough Cleansing

> ⁷ **Purge me with hyssop, and I shall be clean;**
>   **Wash me, and I shall be whiter than snow.**
> ⁸ **Make me hear joy and gladness,**
>   **That the bones You have broken may rejoice.**
> ⁹ **Hide Your face from my sins,**
>   **And blot out all my iniquities (Ps. 51.7-9).**

The earnestness of David's plea for cleansing is manifested in his repetition. It is not enough that he ask once for forgiveness; he feels compelled to ask again and again. This time he says, 'Purge me with hyssop and I shall be clean'. To 'purge' is to remove all traces of contamination and defilement. Utilizing figurative language, he asks that he be purged with hyssop. Hyssop is a small bushy plant, an herb, which was used in purification ceremonies. The bush was dipped in the blood of the sacrifice, which was then sprinkled upon the person or object that needed to be purified. It was first used on the day of Passover, when the Israelites dipped the hyssop in the blood of the sacrificial lamb and applied the blood onto the doorpost and to the top of the door (Exod. 12.22). Later on, when Moses confirmed God's covenant with the people at Mount Sinai, he took the sacrificial blood, dipped the hyssop in the blood, and sprinkled it upon the people as confirmation (Exod. 24.8). The hyssop here is a symbol of cleansing because it is used to apply the blood of cleansing. David's request, 'purge me with hyssop', is a figure of speech, because it is not the hyssop that cleanses his sins; rather, it is the blood that is on the hyssop that cleanses. So David's prayer here is a reference to the cleansing power of the blood of the sacrifice.

He prays further, 'Wash me and I will be whiter than snow'. Snow is a well-known symbol of purity. Nothing is cleaner than freshly fallen snow. The prophet Isaiah utilized the same symbol when he wrote, 'Come now, and let us reason together, saith the LORD: though your sins be as scarlet, they shall be as white as snow; though they be red like crimson, they shall be as wool' (Isa. 1.18).

The psalmist then asks, 'Make me hear joy and gladness' (v. 9). David's guilt has robbed him of joy. The weight of his sin prevents him from enjoying the usual pleasures of life and the spiritual blessings that come in times of worship. David again asks for forgiveness, this time saying to God, 'Hide your face from my sins, and blot out my iniquity'.

David shows in vv. 6-9 that he desires more than just forgiveness. He asked to be forgiven; then, he asks to be clean. In other words, beyond being freed from the *penalty* of sin, he wants to be cleansed from the *presence* of sin. We should not be satisfied to say that we are forgiven and that we will escape hell, which is the penalty for sin. God intends for us a life of fullness and joy in his presence. We should desire to be clean before God, to be pure in heart. Jesus died on the cross to forgive us of our sins but also to 'redeem us from all iniquity and purify' us as his special people (Titus 2.14). The Lord promised this cleansing when he spoke through the prophet Ezekiel: 'Then will I sprinkle clean water upon you, and ye shall be clean: from all your filthiness, and from all your idols, will I cleanse you' (Ezekiel 36.25). Let us pray for complete cleansing from sin.

A Plea for Inner Renewal

 ¹⁰ Create in me a clean heart, O God,
   And renew a steadfast spirit within me.
¹¹ Do not cast me away from Your presence,
   And do not take Your Holy Spirit from me.
¹² Restore to me the joy of Your salvation,
   And uphold me by Your generous Spirit (Ps. 51.10-12).

In the Bible, the word 'create' is used only with God as the subject. Only God can create. We may try to reform the heart, turn the heart, appeal to the heart, and teach the heart; but only God can create a clean heart. David's request for a clean heart points to Jeremiah's prophecy of the new covenant.

> Behold, the days come, saith the LORD, that I will make a new covenant with the house of Israel, and with the house of Judah … I will put my law in their inward parts, and write it in their hearts; and will be their God, and they shall be my people … for I will forgive their iniquity, and I will remember their sin no more (Jeremiah 31.31-34).

Ezekiel uttered a similar prophecy regarding God's plan to create a new heart in his people.

> A new heart also will I give you, and a new spirit will I put within you: and I will take away the stony heart out of your flesh, and I will give you an heart of flesh. And I will put my Spirit within you … and ye shall be my people, and I will be your God (Ezekiel 36.26-28).

God promises more than forgiveness and more than cleansing; he promises the creation of a new heart. God promises to give his people a new heart that loves God, a new heart that desires to serve God. It is a heart that will be filled with God's Spirit. It will be the fulfillment of David's prayer in v. 10, 'create in me a steadfast spirit'.

Then in v. 11, David pleads, 'Do not cast me away from your presence'. Here, he asks for a restored relationship. David, of course, knew what happened to King Saul. When Saul continued to behave in defiance to God's clear directions, God rejected him as king; and the Spirit of the Lord left him. When the Spirit of the Lord departed from him and an evil spirit came upon him, Saul virtually lost his mind, and he became mentally unstable. David's prayer suggests that he may have been thinking about Saul's failure, and he may have been hoping that God would not reject him as well. Therefore, he prays, 'Do not take your Holy Spirit from me'. There is nothing more tragic than a person who was once filled with God's Spirit but now is empty because the Spirit has departed. It is a terrible thing to lose touch with God.

A Promise to Testify

> [13] **Then I will teach transgressors Your ways,**
>   **And sinners shall be converted to You.**
> [14] **Deliver me from the guilt of bloodshed, O God,**
>   **The God of my salvation,**
>   **And my tongue shall sing aloud of Your righteousness.**
> [15] **O Lord, open my lips,**
>   **And my mouth shall show forth Your praise (Ps. 51.13-15).**

Having confessed his sins thoroughly and having repented deeply, David begins to look forward. He says, 'Then …' When he is forgiven, *then* he will teach others. When he is cleansed, *then* sinners will be converted. Once the joy has been restored to him, *then* he will praise God. After God has created in him a new heart, *then* he will use his voice to bless other people. After he has been delivered from the 'guilt of bloodshed', *then* he will 'sing aloud' of God's righteousness. *Then*, he says, 'my mouth will show forth your praise.'

Brokenness and Sacrifice

> [16] **For You do not desire sacrifice, or else I would give it;**
>   **You do not delight in burnt offering.**
> [17] **The sacrifices of God are a broken spirit,**
>   **A broken and a contrite heart –**
>   **These, O God, You will not despise.**
> [18] **Do good in Your good pleasure to Zion;**

Build the walls of Jerusalem.
¹⁹ **Then You shall be pleased with the sacrifices**
    of righteousness,
With burnt offering and whole burnt offering;
Then they shall offer bulls on Your altar (Ps. 51.1-2).

David knows that sacrifices are not sufficient to forgive sins. David understands that the Old Testament sacrifices were an outward symbol of inward faith and repentance. The Old Testament did not teach salvation through the sacrifices, as some people have mistakenly taught. God required that the sacrifice be accompanied by faith and true repentance. The Apostle Paul argued in Romans that the Old Testament believers were justified *by faith* just as we are (Gen. 15.6). The sacrifices were meant to represent a person's repentance and to look forward to the sacrifice of Jesus on the cross. The book of Hebrews explains that the Old Testament sacrifices did not put away sin and did not cleanse the conscience. The sacrifices only *represented* forgiveness. The person was still required to repent. David, therefore, argues that God does not really demand sacrifice and burnt offerings. David knows that what God really wants in us is a broken spirit, a broken and a contrite heart.

Only the Spirit of God can break our hearts so that we can turn to God. True repentance is more than a matter of our will; it is more than a matter of our making a decision in our mind. Of course, the will and the mind are involved in repentance, but the Holy Spirit must draw us to God. Jesus said, 'No one can come to me, except the Father who has sent me draw him' (Jn 6.44). It is the Father, through the Holy Spirit, who draws us to the Savior. Whenever we feel the Holy Spirit tugging at us to draw closer to God, we must not resist. When the Spirit draws us, that is the time to respond.

Finally, the psalm closes with a prayer that God will strengthen the walls of Jerusalem, the holy city. After the city is secured, God will 'be pleased with the sacrifices of righteousness, with burnt offering and whole burnt offering; then they shall offer bulls' on the altar of the temple (v. 19). Most Bible scholars tell us that these last two verses were added to the psalm after the Babylonian captivity when Jerusalem had been destroyed and there was no temple. In that period of time, like today, they could not offer sacrifices. Today, the Jews do not offer sacrifices, because they do not have a temple. So these last two verses are essentially a prayer to God that he will bring about the rebuilding of the temple on Mount Zion and that he will bring about the restoration of the sacrifices.

These last two verses do not stand in contradiction to David's previous statement that God does not desire sacrifice. We know that David did offer sacrifices (2 Sam. 24.22). Again, we note that Psalm 51 is poetry and that one of the literary devices of poetry is to make a very strong statement in order to prove a point, all the while knowing that it is a hyperbole (that is an intentional exaggeration for emphasis). Therefore, when David says to God, 'you do not desire sacrifice', we understand it to mean that *God does not desire a sacrifice that is detached and separate from genuine repentance.* The sacrifices were meant to facilitate repentance, and they were meant to lead the worshiper to the state of brokenness. David knows that what God wants more than anything is our repentant heart and that the sacrifices are just symbols of that repentant heart.

The Old Testament sacrifices functioned in a manner similar to the way water baptism functions today. We do not believe in baptismal regeneration. That is, we do not believe that water baptism produces the new birth. We do not believe that water baptism alone produces the forgiveness of sins that we need. We believe, however, that along with our repentance and conversion, we should be baptized; because baptism represents our cleansing from sin and our death to the old way of life. Water baptism *represents* conversion, but it does not *produce* conversion. It represents a change of heart. It represents death and resurrection – the resurrection of new life as a Christian. As Paul puts it, anyone who is in Christ Jesus 'is a new creature: old things are passed away; behold, all things are become new' (2 Cor. 5.17). Therefore, in a way similar to David's prayer, we might say to God, 'Lord, you do not desire water baptism; you desire genuine repentance'. Still, God commands that we be baptized. In Old Testament times, God still wanted the sacrifices, although his ultimate aim was in the creation of a new heart. Of course, animal sacrifices are not a part of the new covenant, but we still offer sacrifices. What is our sacrifice? Our sacrifices are twofold: first, we present our 'bodies a living sacrifice' (Rom. 12.1); second, we offer 'the sacrifice of praise to God continually' (Heb. 13.15).

Psalm 51 is a powerful example of confession and repentance. If we have anything in our lives that we need to confess to God, David's words can be a model for us to follow in reaching out to God for his grace and mercy. We must allow the Holy Spirit to work in our lives, and we must pray for every obstruction between us and God to be removed. Then, when our hearts have been cleansed by God's grace, we can enter into his presence and worship him in Spirit and in truth.

Conclusion

We have now studied three psalms of lament: Psalm 13, Psalm 22, and Psalm 51. We noted several characteristics of the laments that are present in Psalm 51. First, the laments normally speak directly to God, just as David does here. He prays, 'Be gracious to me, O God'.

Second, we also observed that the lament expresses the pain of abandonment, a theme that is registered in David's words, 'Do not cast me away from your presence, and do not take your Holy Spirit from me. Restore to me the joy of your salvation' (vv. 11-12). To be cast away from God's presence and to be void of God's Spirit would surely signify utter abandonment. David's prayer that he might again 'hear joy and gladness' suggests that he is living in misery because God has cut him off from his presence.

Third, we pointed out that the lament will name the complaint, the problem, the burden. In Psalm 51 the complaint, the problem, is David's sin and its resultant guilt and distress.

Fourth, the lament pleads for God's intervention through the use of specific petitions. This element of the lament is found throughout Psalm 51. David asks that his sins be forgiven, that his heart be cleansed, and that his relationship with God be restored.

Fifth, the lament flows out of a trusting relationship, and usually there is a statement of confidence or trust. Oddly enough, there is no explicit statement of confidence or trust in this psalm. However, David implies trust when he prays on the basis of God's 'lovingkindness'. Therefore, he is trusting in God's lovingkindness, which signifies God's covenant faithfulness. Further trust is implied in v. 14 when David addresses God as 'God of my salvation'. If God is the God of salvation then it implies confidence and trust.

Sixth, there is usually in the lament a statement of assurance that the psalmist has been heard and that God will answer. A clear statement of assurance is lacking in this psalm. However, David promises that when he is forgiven, 'then' he will teach others. He promises that he will help others to find grace just as he found grace.

Seventh, the lament normally concludes with a commitment to praise God, which is found here in vv. 13-15.

Although several of the elements of the lament are not conspicuous in Psalm 51, we should not be surprised. As we pointed out earlier, the writers of the Psalms, while utilizing some standard formulations, were free to express their prayers and their praises in individual ways. The parts of the lament that are not as distinct here as they are in other psalms may be lacking because this psalm, almost from the first word to the last, is permeated by a plea for forgiveness and restoration. It is almost totally a prayer. In its nineteen verses, David utters fifteen requests. Most of the laments devote no more than one or two verses to the specific petitions. However, the plea for forgiveness in Psalm 51 is repeated over and over. David's request for forgiveness is passionate, deep, and urgent; therefore, repetition is necessary. His guilt weighs heavily upon his mind and heart; and this prayer of repentance is in part a means of working through the process of self-examination and self-criticism until he reaches a place of complete honesty and openness with God.

The psalmist is serious about confessing his sin, because sin is a serious matter. Alienation from God is not a matter to be taken lightly. The prayer of Psalm 51 is not generated out of duty or out of daily habit; rather, it pours forth from a heart that is crushed by the effects of sinful choices. It is not a 'now I lay me down to sleep' type of prayer. The psalmist understands the severity of his sin and suffers its distressful consequences. He knows that he has done wrong, and he wants God to know that he is truly, honestly, and deeply repentant.

In the complaint section of the laments, there is usually a complaint against God himself, such as 'How long will you forget me, O Lord?' (Ps. 13.1) or 'My God, My God, why have your forsaken me?' (Ps. 22.1). In many laments, there is a complaint of sickness, or a complaint against an enemy; but not here. In Psalm 51 the only enemy is the psalmist himself. His own sin is his greatest problem. David is his own worst enemy.

Ultimately, we are to blame for the choices we make. We are responsible for the path that we take. We are the only ones who can choose to do right or to do wrong. Therefore, our problem may not be with God, with sickness, with trials, or with enemies. Our most severe battle is the battle inside us, within our hearts. That truth makes Psalm 51 very powerful.

Connecting with the Psalm

(Questions for discussion)

What are some of the excuses that Christians make in order to justify themselves and their sins?

What are important elements in a genuine prayer of repentance?

What is the basis for God's forgiveness of sin? Why does he forgive us?

What would cause God to take away his Holy Spirit from us?

Psalm 51 is an individual prayer, but is there a place for corporate repentance? (See 2 Chron. 7.14 and Rev. 2.1–3.19).

What if ... ?

(Creative and imaginative ideas)

What if we stop making excuses for our sins and, instead, confess them plainly to God?

What if we make it a practice to daily seek for purity of heart and life? (Read Heb. 12.14.)

What if we find a trusted friend who can keep us accountable for our behavior?

What if we testify frequently regarding God's abundant grace?

Now, come up with your own 'What if ... ?'

7

THE PASSIONATE PURSUIT OF GOD'S GLORY: PSALM 63

Setting the Direction

Have you ever experienced the glory of God? When I use the term 'glory of God', I am referring to the manifestation of God's awesome presence. God's glory has been manifested visibly through fire (Exod. 3.2), smoke (Isa. 6.4), a rainbow (Ezek. 1.28), or a cloud (1 Kgs 8.11). Moses and the Israelites witnessed God's glory on Mt. Sinai (Exod. 24.16); and many years later, God's glory descended in similar fashion on the temple that Solomon had built and dedicated to the Lord (2 Chron. 7.1-3). Similarly, Christians throughout history have testified to seeing visible manifestations of God's glory, especially during times of great revival. For example, an eyewitness in Meridian, MS, states, 'While Brother Harris was bringing his message ..., the glory cloud of God came down'.[2] A report from the Church of God Camp Meeting in Somerset, PA, declares, 'the glory of the Lord filled the tabernacle ... the glory-cloud hung low ... The Lord would come down and refresh our souls as the Shekinah glory would fill the place. Is there anything more wonderful than to sit in His divine presence?'[3]

---

[2] *Christ's Ambassadors Herald* (July 1943), p. 13.
[3] *Church of God Evangel* (Sept. 25, 1943), p. 12. For other examples, see *The Pentecostal Evangel* (Dec. 5, 1931), p. 1, and *The Latter Rain Evangel* (May 1939), p. 8.

The prophets Isaiah and Ezekiel saw the glory of the Lord in Spirit-inspired visions (Isaiah 6 and Ezekiel 1-3). In Isaiah's vision, he heard the mighty seraphim cry out,

Holy, holy, holy is the LORD of hosts;
    The whole earth is full of His glory! (Isa. 6.3).

The words of the seraphim suggest that God's glory may not always be visible to everyone; but it is there, nevertheless. As believers, we desire to see God's glory, to recognize it, and to appreciate it. The psalmist David loved God's glory, desired God's glory, and yearned for God's glory to be manifested. He prayed, 'And let the whole earth be filled with His glory' (Ps. 72.19). At its heart, David's prayer restates the request that we find in the Lord's prayer that asks,

Our Father in heaven,
Hallowed be Your name.
Your kingdom come.
Your will be done
On earth as it is in heaven (Mt. 6.9-10).

When God's kingdom comes in its fullness, then God's glory will be clearly seen throughout the earth.

The clearest and most important manifestation of God's glory came to us through God's personal appearance in human form. We read in the Gospel of John, 'And the Word became flesh and dwelt among us, and we beheld His glory, the glory as of the only begotten of the Father, full of grace and truth' (Jn 1.14). Jesus Christ revealed the glory of God in several ways. He revealed God's glory through signs and wonders (Jn 2.11; 11.40). He also revealed God's glory through the 'grace and truth' of his life and his teachings (Jn 1.14). The grace and truth of Jesus reminds us of God's revelation to Moses many hundreds of years earlier. Moses prayed earnestly to God, saying, 'Please, show me Your glory' (Exod. 33.18). In answer to Moses' request, the Lord revealed the depths of divine grace and truth. The Lord said, 'I will make all My goodness pass before you, and I will proclaim the name of the LORD before you. I will be gracious to whom I will be gracious, and I will have compassion on whom I will have compassion' (Exod. 33.19). God's glory was displayed to Moses in the form of grace and compassion.

We, too, desire to see God's glory; and, like the biblical characters, we may experience the glory in a variety of ways. Like Moses, we can see the divine glory in God's grace and compassion. Also, like Isaiah and Ezekiel, we may have dreams and visions in which we experience God's glory. After all, the promise of Pentecost is that 'Your young men shall see visions, Your old men shall dream dreams' (Acts 2.17). Furthermore, like Jesus' disciples, we can see God's glory in the signs and wonders that Jesus continues to perform in the midst of his church today.

If we desire to experience God's glory, then we must seek after God. Moses said, 'you will seek the LORD your God, and you will find Him if you seek Him with all your heart and with all your soul' (Deut. 4.29). As we seek God, we must believe that he desires to reveal his glory to us. We can trust his promise that says, 'Draw near to God and He will draw near to you' (Jas 4.8). The Apostle Paul, speaking about his own passionate pursuit of God's glory, writes,

> that I may know Him and the power of His resurrection … Brethren, I do not count myself to have apprehended; but one thing I do, forgetting those things which are behind and reaching forward to those things which are ahead, I press toward the goal for the prize of the upward call of God in Christ Jesus (Phil. 3.10-14).

Let us emulate the Apostle Paul, and let us seek 'to know' Christ more fully as we 'press toward the goal'.

Discussion Starters

How were Moses and the Israelites affected by seeing the glory of God?

How were Isaiah and Ezekiel affected by their visions of God's glory?

How do healings, miracles, and spiritual gifts bear witness to God's glory today?

Describe your most powerful experience of the glory of God.

Hearing the Word of God

Psalm 63

A Psalm of David when he was in the wilderness of Judah.
[1] O God, You are my God;
  Early will I seek You;
My soul thirsts for You;
  My flesh longs for You
In a dry and thirsty land
  Where there is no water.
[2] So I have looked for You in the sanctuary,
  To see Your power and Your glory.
[3] Because Your lovingkindness is better than life,
  My lips shall praise You.
[4] Thus I will bless You while I live;
  I will lift up my hands in Your name.
[5] My soul shall be satisfied as with marrow and fatness,
  And my mouth shall praise You with joyful lips.
[6] When I remember You on my bed,
  I meditate on You in the night watches.
[7] Because You have been my help,
  Therefore in the shadow of Your wings I will rejoice.
[8] My soul follows close behind You;
  Your right hand upholds me.
[9] But those who seek my life, to destroy it,
  Shall go into the lower parts of the earth.
[10] They shall fall by the sword;
  They shall be a portion for jackals.
[11] But the king shall rejoice in God;
  Everyone who swears by Him shall glory;
    But the mouth of those who speak lies
    shall be stopped.

Introduction

In my first semester at Bible college, I began reading through the entire Bible. As might be expected, a number of Scripture passages made a deep impression upon me; and one of those was Psalm 63, particularly the first two verses:

My soul thirsts for You;
　My flesh longs for You …
So I have looked for You in the sanctuary,
　To see Your power and Your glory.

Psalm 63 is a passionate prayer, an articulation of deep spiritual long-ing; and I saw it as an example of Pentecostal spirituality. In the psalmist's request, I heard an expression of intense desire to encoun-ter God and to experience God's power and glory. The longing for God expressed in Psalm 63 represents to me the passionate pursuit of God that is generated by Pentecostal spirituality, a spirituality that Steven Jack Land has characterized as 'a passion for the kingdom', which is 'ultimately a passion for God' (Land, pp. 2, 97). Because of the content of the psalm and its passionate tone of expression, I memorized the psalm and began to recite it regularly as a part of my own prayers.

Psalm 63 can be divided into four major sections: (1) Longing for God's Presence (vv. 1-2), in which David expresses an unquenchable thirst to see God's power and glory; (2) Praise for God's Kindness (vv. 3-5), which is permeated by a mood of joy and thankfulness; (3) Remembrance of God's Faithfulness (vv. 6-8), which expresses thankfulness but is a thankfulness that leads to expressions of deep trust and commitment to God; and (4) Rejoicing in God's Covenant Protection (vv. 9-11), which reveals a mood of confident hope for the future.

Longing for God's Presence

A Psalm of David when he was in the wilderness of Judah.
¹ O God, You are my God;
　Early will I seek You;
My soul thirsts for You;
　My flesh longs for You
In a dry and thirsty land
　Where there is no water.
² So I have looked for You in the sanctuary,
　To see Your power and Your glory (Ps. 63.1-2).

A passion for God is evident in the first words of the psalmist: 'God, you are my God'. The entire psalm, therefore, is grounded upon Da-vid's personal relationship with God. God had said to Israel, 'I will be your God and you will be my people' (Lev. 26.12). The relationship is one of covenant. Therefore, if we desire to see God's glory manifested in our midst, we must start with our relationship with God. Every day, when we wake up, we should say, 'Oh, God you are my God today'. He is not just the God of David, he is our God. He is not just the God of the pastor, he is our God. He is not just the God of the evangelist, he is our God. He is my God and your God. We can come into his presence to worship him.

Because God is his God, David determines that he will seek God 'early' (v. 1). The Hebrew word translated 'early' means 'dawn' and it means 'to seek with one's whole heart' (Dahood, p. 96), and to 'seek longingly, wholeheartedly, desperately' (Clines, p. 456). When David says that he will seek God early, he implies that prayer is a necessity and a priority. David is not just talking about the time of day, because we know that David also prayed at noontime, in the evening, and even in the middle of the night (Ps. 55.17; 119.62). Therefore, the time of day is not what is important – what is important is the priority of prayer. If you seek him at 6 o'clock in the morning, God will hear you. If you seek him at 8 o'clock in the evening, God will still hear you. Seeking God is not a luxury. It is not an option. To seek God must be our priority.

David's longing for God is made more vivid through the yearning cry, 'My soul thirsts for You; My flesh longs for You'. The language of hunger and thirst creates a mood of intensity in the psalm, and the combination of 'soul' and 'flesh' signifies that the whole person is involved in the longing. The longing of body and soul speaks of a desire that is satisfied with nothing less than God himself and that is prepared to wait patiently for God.

The psalmist's level of yearning is equal to that of 'a dry and thirsty land Where there is no water'. Although the reference to the 'dry and thirsty land' is probably symbolic, it nevertheless provides a vivid image that would be readily identifiable to the original Palestinian hearers of the psalm. It recalls a similar statement found earlier in the Psalter:

As the deer pants for the water brooks,
    So my soul pants for you, O God.
My soul thirsts for God, for the living God' (Ps. 42.1-2).

David longs, body and soul, for his God. He longs deeply and passionately for God's presence, a presence that he has experienced in the past. The absence of God is even more painful given the memory of previous joyful times in the 'sanctuary', among the people of God. In God's holy place, says the psalmist, 'I have looked for you, To see Your power and Your glory'.

God's people desire to be in God's presence. On the one hand, we know that God is present everywhere and that he is always with us. On the other hand, there are times when God's presence is manifested in especially powerful ways. We long for those times of encounter with God. In other psalms, David expresses a similar desire to be in God's presence. He says,

> One thing I have desired of the Lord,
>   That will I seek:
> That I may dwell in the house of the Lord
>   All the days of my life,
> To behold the beauty of the Lord,
>   And to inquire in His temple (Ps. 27.4).

David prays that he might dwell in the house of the Lord all the days of his life, to 'behold the beauty of the LORD, and to inquire in His temple'. His statement indicates that the worship of God is his greatest joy. To dwell in the house of the Lord means to remain there at all times. To behold the beauty of the Lord means to see God in all his glory. 'Blessed are the pure in heart for they shall see God' (Mt. 5.8).

The deepest desire of God's people is to dwell in the house of the Lord. The same sentiment is found in Ps. 23.6, where David announces, 'I will dwell in the house of the Lord forever' and in Psalm 84, where he cries out,

> My soul longs, yes, even faints
>   For the courts of the LORD;
>   My heart and my flesh cry out for the living God …
> Blessed are those who dwell in Your house;
>   They will still be praising You (Ps. 84.2-4).[4]

---

[4] See also Psalms 5.8; 23.6; 26.8; 36.9; 42.5; 52.10; 55.15, 65.5; 66.13; 84.11; etc.

The one thing that David especially desires is to be in the house of God. It is there among the people of God that David can enjoy the Lord's presence, behold the Lord's beauty, and seek God's face. David writes, 'In Your presence is fullness of joy' (Ps. 16.11). To be in the house of God is his constant passion; it is the goal and object of his life. In his role as the King of Israel, David would have faced any number of daily challenges that would have occupied his time. Nevertheless, he chose to make attendance to the house of God one of his highest priorities. Similarly, the early church exhibited a deep desire for constant worship and prayer. Luke reports that the early believers who were newly filled with the spirit continued 'with one accord in the temple' (Acts 2.46). The example of David and of the early church should encourage us to evaluate our own priorities. In our technological age, we are tempted to relegate the house of God to an afterthought while we are busy pursuing entertainment, pleasure, and affluence.

When David returns to the house of God, he expects to witness God's 'power and glory'. God's 'power' is his sovereign capacity to choose, to act, and to intervene in the world (for both judgment and salvation). His 'glory' is the display of his weightiness, his awesomeness, his majesty, and his holiness. The seeing of God and the beholding of God's power and glory refer to an encounter with God, an experience of God's presence which David had enjoyed on earlier occasions.

The psalmist's experience of 'seeing' God and 'beholding' the power and glory of God are signs to Pentecostals that God is open to human encounter. Pentecostal worshipers expect to encounter God. This expectation undergirds much of our worship and theology and may even be identified as another way of defining worship. From Azusa Street until now, Pentecostals everywhere have insisted upon the present reality of God's presence to save, sanctify, fill with the Holy Spirit, heal, and reign as coming king.

The psalmist's longing for the manifestation of God's 'power and glory' provides biblical justification for Pentecostalism's passionate pursuit of God. This longing for God is described repeatedly in early Pentecostal literature. For example, Alice Flower writes, 'All I seemed to sense was a deep craving for the overflowing of His love in my heart. At that moment it seemed I wanted Jesus more than anything in all the world.'[5] Reflecting on her passion for God, Zelma E. Argue recalls, 'my whole heart seemed to be just one big vacuum craving and crying for God' (in Blumhofer, p. 159). Echoing the words of Ps. 63.6, Alice E. Luce affirms, 'the Lord is our portion. We have had a real taste of the Lord and found out that he is a satisfying portion' (in Blumhofer, p. 136).

Praise for God's Kindness

[3] **Because Your lovingkindness is better than life,**
  My lips shall praise You.
[4] **Thus I will bless You while I live;**
  I will lift up my hands in Your name.
[5] **My soul shall be satisfied as with marrow and fatness,**
  And my mouth shall praise You with joyful lips
  (Ps. 63.3-5).

Immediately after his prayer for God's presence, David breaks forth in joyous praise. 'My lips shall praise You', he declares to God, 'Because Your lovingkindness is better than life'. The word 'lovingkindness' is a translation of the word *ḥesed,* a word that is difficult to explain with a single English term. As explained earlier, the Hebrew *ḥesed* refers to God's love, loyalty, faithfulness, kindness, and mercy that come to the believer because of God's covenant. It is God's unbreakable commitment to his covenant. Therefore, David is saying that God's covenant commitment to his people is more precious than life itself.

David's statement is unique in the Old Testament. Normally, the Old Testament presents lovingkindness as God's blessing upon the believer's life. Here, however, God's lovingkindness is greater than life itself. Thus, David suggests that God's lovingkindness can be experienced separate and apart from life in this present world. David's bold assertion implies that God's lovingkindness continues even after this life is ended. Even death cannot separate us from God's covenant faithfulness, his *ḥesed.* The statement is David's attempt to express the inexpressible wonder of God's covenant faithfulness.

In celebration of God's faithful love, the psalmist pledges to 'praise' God, to 'bless' God, and to 'lift up' his hands to God in

---

[5] *Assemblies of God Heritage* 20 (Winter 1997-98), p. 18.

worship. Lifting up the hands was the customary attitude of the wor-shipper in prayer. It was a sign of an expectant trust that the wor-shiper's empty hands will be filled with divine blessings. This praise will not be offered briefly or intermittently; it will continue through-out the psalmist's life. He promises to bless the Lord in perpetual worship.

Like David, we must praise God for his faithfulness; and we must seek after God, because he is faithful. We long for God, because we want to experience his faithfulness; and we hunger for God, because we know he is faithful. Thus, we must praise him for his faithfulness and lift up our hands in worship.

The mood of exuberant jubilation is reinforced with the state-ment, 'My soul shall be satisfied as with marrow and fatness'. The phrase, 'Marrow and fatness', signifies very rich food, especially the sumptuous foods that were enjoyed in the annual Jewish feasts. Therefore, the psalmist anticipates a great feast but not literally. He says that being in God's presence is 'like' a great feast; therefore, he is speaking of a spiritual feast, not a physical feast. Thus, David again imagines the blessings of God to be distinct from the material world. The lovingkindness of God is like a sumptuous feast that quenches the thirst and satisfies the hunger. Because of God's kindness, the psalmist can look forward to a full and joyous life; and because he is blessed, his mouth will offer praise 'with joyful lips' (v. 5).

Remembrance of God's Faithfulness

⁶ **When I remember You on my bed,**
   I meditate on You in the night watches.
⁷ **Because You have been my help,**
   Therefore in the shadow of Your wings I will rejoice.
⁸ **My soul follows close behind You;**
   Your right hand upholds me (Ps. 63.6-8).

The third section of Psalm 63 continues to express thankfulness, but the tone transitions to a mood of deep trust and commitment to God. This passage recalls the past benefits of David's relationship to God. The psalmist asserts that just as God has been faithful to him, he has been faithful to God by remembering God and meditating upon God, two activities that signal deep devotion and commitment.

The psalmist remembers that, with God as his 'help', he shouted for joy underneath the covering of God's 'wings', which represent God's protection. He remembers further that he followed 'close behind' God and that God supported him. The phrase, 'My soul follows close behind You', is a loose translation from the Hebrew. The Hebrew says literally, 'My soul stuck to your back!' The verb 'stuck' (Hebrew, *davaq*) means 'to cling, cleave, stick to' (cf. Gen. 2.24). Metaphorically, it signifies 'loyalty, affection, etc.' (*BDB*, p. 179). Israel is commanded to 'stick' to the Lord (Deut. 10.20; 13.5; Josh. 23.8; Ps. 119.31). While the psalmist 'stuck close' to God, God 'upheld' him with his powerful 'right hand'. David's testimony indicates that if we will stick close to God, God will provide support and help whenever we need it. We are reminded of the promise of Jesus, who says, 'If you abide in Me, and My words abide in you, you will ask what you desire, and it shall be done for you' (Jn 15.7).

Some people follow God afar off, but David followed God closely. Moses commanded Israel saying, 'You shall fear the LORD your God; you shall serve Him, and to Him you shall hold fast' (Deut. 10.20). We must 'hold fast' to God and cling to him. We must wrap our arms around God and not let go.

As we seek after God, as we worship God, and as we praise God, we must remember God's works in the past. We must remember what God has done, and we must share our testimony. We must be always ready to say, 'This is what the Lord has done for me'. Let us remember when the Lord saved us. Let us remember when the Lord filled us with the Holy Spirit. Let us remember the times when the Lord healed us. Let us remember when he answered our prayers. Let us remember those times of God's faithfulness and blessing.

The psalmist feels that he will die of hunger and thirst unless God appears with his refreshing presence. In our practice of the Pentecostal life, we must become hungry and thirsty for God, desperate for God's presence. In many cases, however, our desperation for God's presence and help has been supplanted by structures of our own invention, substitutes for the power and glory of God. In the prophecies of Jeremiah, the Lord warned his people to avoid substitutes. He says, 'For My people have committed two evils: They have forsaken Me, the fountain of living waters, And hewn themselves cisterns – broken cisterns that can hold no water' (Jer. 2.13). Like the people of Jeremiah's day, we have learned how to do 'church' without God. Consequently, prayers of desperation are rarely heard, because we have backup plans, safety nets, and formal structures that can exist without God's help. May God help us to cry out that his glory would be manifested in our midst.

Rejoicing in God's Covenant Protection

> **⁹ But those who seek my life, to destroy it,**
>   **Shall go into the lower parts of the earth.**
> **¹⁰ They shall fall by the sword;**
>   **They shall be a portion for jackals.**
> **¹¹ But the king shall rejoice in God;**
>   **Everyone who swears by Him shall glory;**
> **But the mouth of those who speak lies**
>   **shall be stopped (Ps. 63.9-11).**

This final section of the psalm displays a mood of confident hope for the future. The passage unfolds through a contrast between the psalmist's enemies and 'the king' (v. 11). The enemies, who seek 'to destroy' the psalmist, will 'go into the lower parts of the earth', and they will become 'a portion for jackals'. The king, however, will rejoice in God, along with all those who swear allegiance to God, because the mouths of the deceivers 'shall be stopped'.

The psalmist is confident that justice will prevail, that evil will be punished, and that God's people 'shall glory' in their covenant relationship with God. Wicked enemies, struck down by 'the sword', will receive their due punishment. They will be deprived of a proper burial, and their dead bodies will be desecrated by wild animals. In the end, those who seek to destroy God's people will themselves be destroyed.

The king, however, will 'rejoice in God'; and those who swear allegiance to God will 'glory'. The phrase 'Everyone who swears by Him' is a poetic description of the Israelites. Therefore, it is the psalmist's way of connecting the psalm to the community of faith.

The last section of Psalm 63 is a fitting conclusion to the psalm. The psalmist has declared his sense of separation from God's presence (v. 1) and his need to be satisfied by God's kindness (v. 5). He has remembered (v. 6) times when he needed God's help (v. 7) and when God came to his aid. In this final passage, David recognizes the ongoing presence of dangerous enemies who threaten his safety. Nevertheless, his past experiences of God's presence (v. 2), God's covenant loyalty (v. 3), and God's tender care (v. 8) have generated a renewed confidence in God's faithfulness. The psalmist is convinced that God's people will prevail in the end.

These final verses of Psalm 63 imply that we must reaffirm our hope in the Lord's soon return. This last section points to the future and could even be considered as a reference to the last days. At the return of Jesus, the wicked will be punished; those who are faithful to God will rejoice in God's protection; and the kingdom of God will manifest itself as a kingdom of justice and righteousness.

Conclusion to Psalm 63

The four sections of Psalm 63 are held together by two parallel threads that span the entire psalm. The first thread consists of David's affirmations about God. He says that God is his God (v. 1); that God's covenant kindness is greater than life (v. 3); that God will satisfy the psalmist's desires (v. 5); that God has been the psalmist's help (v. 7) and support (v. 8); and that God will destroy the psalmist's enemies (vv. 9, 10, 11). The second thread consists of statements that describe David's response to God. These responses can be summarized in two categories: seeking God (v. 1) and praising God (vv. 3, 4, 5, 7, 11). We may also infer that the psalmist's past actions are appropriate for both the present and the future. These past responses are remembering God (v. 6), meditating upon God (v. 6), and sticking close to God (v. 8).

Implications of Psalm 63

I would suggest the following ways in which Psalm 63 can help to shape our spirituality, both now and in the future. These implications are only suggestive, and they are meant to promote discussion and prayer.

First, Pentecostals face the danger of seeking out experiences rather than seeking God for God's sake. In the past, Pentecostals called this kind of shallow emotionalism 'wild fire'. It is all too easy for worship to become no more than entertainment or self-gratification.

The manifestation of God's holy presence cannot be manipulated by ministers and worship leaders who prompt and prod the congregation until they are worked up emotionally. The disciples' encounter with God through the Holy Spirit in Acts 2 was powerful and moving, but it did not occur as a result of their own artificial efforts. In response to their prayer, their worship, and their waiting, the Holy Spirit came upon them as an external force sent from heaven. Similarly, the focus of Psalm 63 is upon the relational quality of the encounter between the psalmist and God. Likewise for us, we must worship God and welcome God's response to our worship.

Second, Pentecostalism must recover the practice of testimony. Psalm 63 is directed to God, but it is a song that is meant to be heard by the congregation; and as such, it functions as testimony. The psalmist testifies to the experience of seeing God's glory in the sanctuary and to the many times when God has been a help and a support. This testimony includes aspects of the psalmist's spiritual journey, such as times of praise, meditation, and sticking close to God. The recounting of the psalmist's own longing for God is an implicit challenge to the hearer to pursue God with the same fervent intensity and with the same unreserved yearning.

Third, if the Pentecostal movement is to maintain its vitality from generation to generation, it must consistently practice and periodically reclaim the spiritual passion that we find demonstrated in Psalm 63. The biblical text functions as a vehicle of spiritual formation that can inform Pentecostal spirituality and practice. If we expect to encounter the presence of God, we must follow David's example and seek God passionately. We believe in the manifestation of God's power – healings, miracles, spiritual gifts, tongues, and prophecy. If we are to see God's power, to experience God's glory, we must seek God wholeheartedly.

Finally, if we want to encounter God, we must expect to be filled. David believed that God would meet his need. He confessed, 'my soul shall be satisfied' (Ps. 63.5). David believed that if he sought God, he would be filled. Other Scriptures assure us that God 'satisfies the longing soul, and fills the hungry soul with goodness' (Ps. 107.9). Jesus gave us the following promise: 'Blessed are those who hunger and thirst for righteousness, for they shall be filled' (Mt. 5.6). We must expect God to fill us as we passionately pursue God's glory!

Connecting with the Psalm

(Questions for discussion)

What are the signs that we have lost our passion for the presence of God?

How can we connect this psalm to Hebrews 10.19-25?

What steps can we take to restore our love for God's glory?

Discuss a time when the Lord was your help and your support.

How do we maintain hope for the future?

Share which part of this psalm gives you the most cause to praise God.

What if ... ?

(Creative and imaginative ideas)

What if we prayerfully evaluate our spiritual desires in light of Psalm 63?

What if we set aside a day for prayer and fasting?

What if we make a list of our blessings and share that list with other people?

What if we extend God's kindness and love to someone who needs help?

Now, come up with your own 'What if ... ?'

8

THE PASSIONATE PURSUIT OF SPIRITUAL PERCEPTION: PSALM 73

Setting the Direction

Have you ever heard anyone say, 'You need to get your head on straight?' Well that is what Psalm 73 is all about – getting our heads on straight. To put it in more theological terms, this psalm presents worship as a pursuit of spiritual perception. That is, worship helps us to see reality as God sees it, not as humans see it.

Spiritual realities are not easily recognized, as Elisha's servant learned when he and Elisha were surrounded by Syrian soldiers. The servant was afraid; and Elisha said, 'Do not fear, for those who are with us are more than those who are with them'. Then Elisha prayed, and the Lord opened the eyes of the servant; and he saw that 'the mountain was full of horses and chariots of fire all around Elisha' (2 Kgs 6.16-17). This story of Elisha and his servant illustrates the existence of different perceptions of reality. The reality seen by Elisha was different from the reality seen by the servant.

We learn from Hebrews 11 that spiritual realities are often invisible to the natural eye. We read that 'faith is the substance of things hoped for and the evidence of things not seen' (Heb. 11.1). If things are 'not seen', can they be real? The answer, of course, is 'Yes, they are real'. Abraham searched for a country and a city that he had never seen (Heb. 11.8-10); and when Moses left Egypt, 'he endured as seeing him who is invisible' (Heb. 11.27).

Psalm 73 demonstrates that when we enter into the presence of God, he changes our perception of reality. Being in the presence of God changes our understanding of what is right and what is wrong, what is good and what is bad. Being in the presence of God changes our perception of who we are in relation to God. In the presence of God, the truth is made known; secrets of the heart are unveiled; wickedness is condemned; lies are exposed; and hypocrisy is judged. Also, in the presence of God, the wounded are healed; the poor are lifted up; the weary are strengthened; the grieving are comforted; and the fearful are encouraged. In the presence of God, our perception of reality is stripped of all pretense; and the truth is made evident. In his presence, God becomes everything, encompassing both the beginning and the end of all things.

Discussion Starters

Discuss some very important topics about which people often disagree. What causes these differences of opinion?

What are some reasons that we fail to see God's perspective?

What are some ways that 'natural' vision is different from 'spiritual' vision?

Hearing the Word of God

Psalm 73

A Psalm of Asaph.
¹ Truly God is good to Israel,
   To such as are pure in heart.
² But as for me, my feet had almost stumbled;
   My steps had nearly slipped.
³ For I was envious of the boastful,
   When I saw the prosperity of the wicked.
⁴ For there are no pangs in their death,
   But their strength is firm.
⁵ They are not in trouble as other men,
   Nor are they plagued like other men.
⁶ Therefore pride serves as their necklace;
   Violence covers them like a garment.
⁷ Their eyes bulge with abundance;
   They have more than heart could wish.
⁸ They scoff and speak wickedly concerning oppression;
   They speak loftily.
⁹ They set their mouth against the heavens,
   And their tongue walks through the earth.
¹⁰ Therefore his people return here,
   And waters of a full cup are drained by them.
¹¹ And they say, 'How does God know?
   And is there knowledge in the Most High?'
¹² Behold, these are the ungodly, Who are always at ease;
   They increase in riches.
¹³ Surely I have cleansed my heart in vain,
   And washed my hands in innocence.
¹⁴ For all day long I have been plagued,
   And chastened every morning.
¹⁵ If I had said, 'I will speak thus,'
   Behold, I would have been untrue to the generation of
   Your children.
¹⁶ When I thought how to understand this,
   It was too painful for me—

¹⁷ Until I went into the sanctuary of God,
Then I understood their end.
¹⁸ Surely You set them in slippery places;
You cast them down to destruction.
¹⁹ Oh, how they are brought to desolation, as in a moment!
They are utterly consumed with terrors.
²⁰ As a dream when one awakes, So, Lord, when You awake,
You shall despise their image.
²¹ Thus my heart was grieved,
And I was vexed in my mind.
²² I was so foolish and ignorant;
I was like a beast before You.
²³ Nevertheless I am continually with You;
You hold me by my right hand.
²⁴ You will guide me with Your counsel,
And afterward receive me to glory.
²⁵ Whom have I in heaven but You?
And there is none upon earth that I desire besides You.
²⁶ My flesh and my heart fail;
But God is the strength of my heart and
my portion forever.
²⁷ For indeed, those who are far from You shall perish;
You have destroyed all those who desert You for harlotry.
²⁸ But it is good for me to draw near to God;
I have put my trust in the Lord GOD,
That I may declare all Your works.

The Heading of Psalm 73

A Psalm of Asaph.

The Psalter is divided into five books, and Psalm 73 is the first psalm in Book Three. Book Two closes with the words, 'The prayers of David the son of Jesse are ended' (Ps. 72.20), thus marking the end of a certain collection of David's psalms, particularly his prayers. That does not mean, however, that there are no more psalms of David in the book of Psalms; it just means that Psalm 72 is the end of one collection of the psalms of David.

Psalm 73 is a psalm of Asaph, who is named in the headings of twelve psalms. Eleven of those twelve psalms are in Book Three of the Psalter; the other is in Book Two (Psalm 50). Asaph is described in 1 Chronicles as a musician who worked in the temple as one of David's worship leaders (6.31-39). He apparently led a group of singers and musicians who were known by the name, 'the sons of Asaph' (1 Chron. 25.1-2).

The Accepted Truth

¹ **Truly God is good to Israel,**
   To such as are pure in heart.

Psalm 73 narrates four steps in a process of growth in the life of the psalmist.

   1. Foundational belief – God is good to his people.
   2. Contradictory observation – The wicked prosper.
   3. Reality revisioned – God will set things straight.
   4. Renewed faith – Asaph will trust in God.

Step one begins with the accepted truth that God is good to Israel and to those who are of a pure heart. Asaph's foundational belief is our belief as well. In step two, the psalmist's established belief is challenged when he sees the prosperity of the wicked. He reasons that if God is good to the pure in heart, if God punishes the wicked, then why is it that the wicked appear to prosper? Step three is Asaph's entrance into the sanctuary of God; and there, the truth of God's goodness to him is renewed. There in the sanctuary of God, he sees the end of the wicked. Finally, in step four, Asaph appropriates the truth to himself. The last verse says, 'It is good for me to draw near to God. I have put my trust in the Lord God'. So, he has come full circle; God is good, and it is good for him to be close to God. It is good for him to be close to God and to trust in the Lord. These are the main points in the psalm, and as we go through this psalm, we can see how the message develops.

The psalm begins with a powerful statement, 'Truly, God is good to Israel, to such as are pure in heart'. We find other verses very similar to this throughout the Old Testament:

'Taste and see that the Lord is good; blessed is the man who trusts in him' (Ps. 34.8);

'For the Lord is good; his mercy is everlasting' (Ps. 100.5);

'Praise the Lord, for the Lord is good' (Ps. 135.3);

'Praise the Lord of hosts for the Lord is good' (Jer. 31.11);

'The Lord is good to those who wait for him' (Lam. 3.25);

'The Lord is good, a stronghold in the day of trouble, and he knows those who trust in him' (Nahum 1.7).

Psalm 1 tells us that the righteous are blessed and the wicked are doomed. The righteous person is 'like a tree planted by the rivers of water', and everything he does will prosper (Ps. 1.3). The wicked, however, are 'like the husk that the wind drives away' (Ps. 1.4); and they have no place in the congregation of the righteous. 'The Lord knows the way of the righteous, but the way of the wicked will perish' (Ps. 1.6). The very first Psalm, therefore, tells us that God will bring wicked people to destruction but that God is watching over his people to take care of them and to bless them. Psalm 73 begins with the same assurance – 'God is good to Israel, To such as are pure in heart'.

The Questioning of Truth

> ² **But as for me, my feet had almost stumbled;**
>   **My steps had nearly slipped.**
> ³ **For I was envious of the boastful,**
>   **When I saw the prosperity of the wicked.**

Asaph believes in God's goodness; but, when he sees wicked people who appear to be doing well, he is troubled. Therefore, he admits that he 'almost stumbled' and that he was 'envious' of the wicked because he saw their prosperity. The Hebrew word for 'prosperity' here is '*shalom*', which means wellness and wholeness. When he observes the wicked, they show all the signs of health, wealth, and happiness. There is no evidence that they are suffering under the judgment of God at all. It looks as if God is blessing them. Of course, this is Asaph's perception. Envy, jealousy, and covetousness are dangerous attitudes that can color our view of reality. We imperil our own spiritual health when we compare ourselves (and our possessions) with other people. It is then that our feet may slip, and we may tumble into the kind of envy that the psalmist talks about here. It is good, however, that the psalmist admits his envy of the wicked and the negative results of that envy. The first step to finding a solution is to admit our need.

Description of the Wicked and Their Prosperity

⁴ **For there are no pangs in their death,**
  But their strength is firm.
⁵ **They are not in trouble as other men,**
  Nor are they plagued like other men.
⁶ **Therefore pride serves as their necklace;**
  Violence covers them like a garment.
⁷ **Their eyes bulge with abundance;**
  They have more than heart could wish.
⁸ **They scoff and speak wickedly concerning oppression;**
  They speak loftily.
⁹ **They set their mouth against the heavens,**
  And their tongue walks through the earth.

Asaph does not stop with his admission of envy toward the wicked. He expands on his description of their abundance, their extravagance, and their pride. In verses four through nine, the psalmist enumerates at least four specific areas where he sees the wicked prospering. First, the wicked do not suffer at their time of death like many of the good people. Apparently, Asaph is arguing that the wicked can afford the best doctors, the finest comforts, and the most expensive food and drink. Perhaps, they have servants to attend to their needs. Because of all these advantages, he does not think they are suffering. This is Asaph's perception of these wicked people.

Second, they are not in 'trouble', neither are they 'plagued' like other people. Because of their wealth, they have no financial problems. They need not worry if the weather will turn bad or if their crops will come up short. They have more than enough. Their fine houses and new clothes will protect them from the cold and from disease. If one of their animals dies, they will hardly miss it.

Third, Asaph speaks of their pride. These wicked people are proud, boastful, and violent. They wear their pride unashamedly like a necklace and their violence covers them like a garment. The theme of pride is picked up again in verses eight and nine. They 'scoff' and 'speak loftily' about their wicked exploits. These evil people take advantage of those who are weaker. They boast in their wickedness.

Furthermore, they are so arrogant that they speak against God himself. They 'set their mouth against the heavens.' They believe they are all-powerful. Asaph does not identify these powerful people; so we have to assume that they are either people in the community who are disobeying God's laws and are oppressing their neighbors, or they are enemies who have invaded Israel, such as the Assyrians and Babylonians.

Fourth, he observes their wealth. He says, 'Their eyes bulge with abundance'. They eat so much that their eyes are popping out. Food was not as abundant in the ancient world as it is in today's Western societies. In biblical times, most of the people barely subsisted from one crop to another, and hunger was a very present reality. If the crops were not abundant, the people faced many difficult months; and some of them might even starve to death. There were no food banks, food stamps, community centers, or welfare programs. Asaph says of the wicked that they have more than their heart could wish. He knows that some righteous people do not have enough; yet, these wicked people have too much.

The Suffering of God's People

> [10] **Therefore his people return here,**
>   **And waters of a full cup are drained by them.**
> [11] **And they say, 'How does God know?**
>   **And is there knowledge in the Most High?'**
> [12] **Behold, these are the ungodly, Who are always at ease;**
>   **They increase in riches.**

Asaph sees the comfortable lives of the wicked, and he sees also the suffering of God's 'people' (v. 10). His statement that 'the waters of a full cup are drained by them' appears strange and cryptic to us. He seems to be saying that God's people are so poor that they could not spare one drop out of a cup of water. They will drink every drop of a cup of water, because they may not get any more. In ancient times, all drinking water would come either from a stream or from a well. Therefore, the bottom of the cup would likely contain a bit of dirt or dregs, which would not be consumed. However, he is saying here that they would drain their cups dry because they are so poor. They do not want to waste even a drop because it is so precious to them.

The Confusion of the psalmist

¹³ **Surely I have cleansed my heart in vain,**
  And washed my hands in innocence.
¹⁴ **For all day long I have been plagued,**
  And chastened every morning.

The psalmist observes the ungodly, always at ease and increasing in riches. He reasons that it is pointless to serve God. 'Surely,' he says, 'I have cleansed my heart in vain and washed my hands in innocence'. In other words, he considers his efforts to serve God to be in vain. He has been faithful to God, but he sees no benefit in his faithfulness. He is doing everything that he can to live according to God's commandments, but he is suffering. His rich neighbors have not obeyed God, and they seem to be blessed. So, what is the point of living for God? The observation of the psalmist seems to be in contradiction to the promise of Psalm 1, where we read that the righteous person is like a tree, planted by rivers of water, which brings forth fruit; his leaf does not wither; and whatsoever he does prospers.

Despite all his efforts to maintain a clean heart and clean hands (which symbolize actions), he continues to be 'chastened every morning' and 'plagued' all day long. Even though he is living faithfully, he feels like he is suffering all the time.

The dilemma of the psalmist in Psalm 73 is a natural human struggle. It is reminiscent of Job's struggle and of the question that Satan proposed in Job 1. When Satan speaks to God about Job, he says, 'Does Job serve God for nothing?' He then says, 'If you will take away all the things that you have given Job he will curse you.' So God allows Satan to take away Job's possessions, his property, and his family. Everything is snatched from Job, but Job does not curse God. Instead Job says, 'The LORD gave and the LORD has taken away, Blessed be the name of the LORD' (Job 1.21). If the Lord gives to us, we should praise him. If he takes it away, we should praise him still. Jesus encourages us to focus upon spiritual things rather than on the material. He says, 'Your life consists of more than the clothes you wear or the food you eat' (Lk. 12.23). Therefore, let us praise him.

Spiritual Perception in God's Presence

¹⁵ **If I had said, 'I will speak thus,'**
   Behold, I would have been untrue to the generation of |
   Your children.
¹⁶ **When I thought how to understand this,**
   It was too painful for me–
¹⁷ **Until I went into the sanctuary of God,**
   Then I understood their end.

Asaph believes that something is wrong with the reality that he observes in the world. Something is wrong when the wicked are prospering and the righteous are suffering. However, he recognizes the possible harmful consequences of voicing his doubts publicly. If he were to speak about his skepticism, he 'would have been untrue to the generation' of God's children. That is, he does not want to discourage other people. Perhaps Asaph writes from the perspective of his role as a leader among the worship leaders. He does not want to discourage the people who are under his leadership. This is a good lesson for those of us who are in leadership and for parents and teachers. Unfortunately, some people seem to enjoy bringing discouragement and gloom wherever they go. There seems to be a dark cloud hovering over their heads. And every time they open their mouth, they suck the life and the joy out of everything. We should not speak everything that comes to our minds, particularly when it may produce detrimental effects on other people. We would be wise to keep some of our thoughts to ourselves. Scripture advises us, 'Do not be rash with your mouth, And let not your heart utter anything hastily before God. For God is in heaven, and you on earth; therefore let your words be few' (Eccl. 5.2). The psalmist is right to be concerned about other people and what effect his words will have upon them.

Asaph is trying to make sense of what he has observed in the world. He is asking himself why the wicked are prospering and why the righteous are suffering. He is troubled by his thoughts. He says, 'When I thought how to understand this, it was too painful for me' (v. 16). His mind could not handle the apparent contradiction. Asaph was not the first nor the last to struggle with these questions. The matter of God's justice and righteousness has been studied by all of the world's greatest philosophers, and none of them has offered a satisfactory conclusion. Books have been written by the hundreds trying to explain why righteous people suffer, but there are some things that we cannot understand.

In his troubled state, Asaph entered the 'sanctuary', the house of God. The psalmist comes into the sanctuary of God seeking for light and for answers to his difficult questions. There, in the presence of God, his understanding is enlightened; and he sees a different picture of the wicked. He finds peace of mind when he sees 'their end'. Asaph does not explain exactly how this transformation happens. He says simply, 'I went into the sanctuary'. The psalmist is talking about the power of worship, the transforming power of being in the presence of God. He is demonstrating and testifying to the fact that encountering God in worship is more than a ritual, more than meaningless habit. The psalmist is telling us that worship causes us to see the world differently. In worship, our entire perspective changes. Asaph went into the sanctuary; then, he understood. We do not know if he heard some kind of teaching, if he heard a prophecy, or if he heard someone reading the Scripture. We do not know if he heard someone praying, or if he heard a praise or a testimony. Perhaps David was there, and David took out his harp and began to sing, 'The Lord is my shepherd; I shall not want, he maketh me to lie down in green pastures. He restores my soul.' Perhaps he heard someone singing Psalm 27, 'The Lord is my light and my salvation, whom shall I fear; the Lord is the strength of my life, of whom shall I be afraid. When my enemies and my foes came upon me to eat up my flesh, they stumbled and fell. Though a host should encamp against me, in this I will be confident.' Whatever happened, it was in the presence of God, as he worshiped before the Lord and as he beheld the beauty of the Lord and the power of the Lord, that God turned him around. He came into the sanctuary depressed, but he went out encouraged. He came in down, but he left with his head held high. He could have contacted the Bible scholars to give him the explanation, but they would have revealed nothing new. There, in the sanctuary of God, however, he received a new view of reality. It was not through any change of the circumstances but through a change of his spiritual understanding, a change of his spiritual location, that he sees the world differently. Being in the presence of God changes our outlook on the world.

Psalm 73 reminds me of Job's experience. Throughout the entire book of Job, he and his 'friends' attempt to determine the reason for Job's suffering. They cannot understand why so many tragedies have befallen him. Job questions God and seeks for explanations. Then, at the end of the book of Job, God appears and begins to reveal his greatness to Job. God says, 'Were you there when I put the stars in place? Were you there when the morning stars sang together?' God expounds upon his majesty, his power, and his glory; and Job says, 'I have heard about you with my ears but now my eyes have seen you, and I repent in dust and ashes' (Job 42.5-6). Job went away from that encounter with God a changed man, a happy man, a satisfied man, a content man. Yet, we notice that God never answered Job's questions. When Job entered the presence of God, the questions no longer seemed so important.

The questions themselves begin to fade into nothingness when we enter into the presence of the Lord. In the book of Revelation, the Apostle John is exiled on the island of Patmos. In a vision, he sees the troubles coming upon the world. But then, God says to John, 'Come up here' (Rev. 4.1). Up he goes to the throne room of God; and from God's throne room, the entire world looks different. There, in the presence of God, John's perspective changes. Similarly, we read in the book of Isaiah that in the year that King Uzziah died, the prophet Isaiah went to the house of God. No doubt he was concerned about the death of the king and the future of the kingdom; but then Isaiah says, 'I saw the Lord, high and lifted up. And his train filled the temple and his glory was everywhere'. Isaiah's encounter with the presence of the Lord changed Isaiah's life.

We might recall the experience of the disciples after Jesus rose from the dead. Jesus visited with them for 40 days, and he told them to wait in Jerusalem until they were clothed with power from heaven. Therefore, they went to the temple to pray and worship; but they were afraid, and they had no direction. Still, they gathered together and waited as the Lord had told them. Then, the day of Pentecost came, and they were all filled with the Holy Spirit. No longer were they afraid, and no longer were they fearful. Immediately, they began to go throughout the land preaching the gospel. Why? It was because they had an encounter with the presence of God that gave clarity to their mind, direction to their life, and purpose for their actions. The threats had not disappeared; in fact, Peter and John were soon arrested and forbidden to preach. When they were released, they returned to the church; and everyone gathered together to pray. There in prayer, the Holy Spirit came down again; and we read that they were all filled with the Holy Spirit, and they spoke the word of God with boldness. They were still under the threats, and many of them gave their lives; but they did not care, because they were in the presence of the Lord. That is the difference it makes when we come into God's house and encounter his presence.

Can you testify to a similar experience? I can. Many times we have faced questions, difficult circumstances, and needed answers. Then, we entered the house of God, and we worshiped God, and we sought God. At some point during that service of worship, God reached out and touched us. He may not have answered our prayers immediately, and he may not have given us answers to all of our questions; but because God came down and touched us, we received a new vision of reality. When we entered the worship, we were at the point of giving up; but we departed with new strength. We came in sick, but we went out healed. In God's presence, this renewal can happen in a moment, in an instant. It can happen in various ways: it can be a song, a Scripture, the sermon, a testimony, a kind word from a member of the congregation, or it can be a prayer. God speaks to us through songs and through the preaching. God speaks to us as we are reading our Bibles. God speaks to us as someone beside us prays for us. Through whatever means it happens, ultimately it is the presence of God in the sanctuary of worship that transforms us. It is God's Holy Spirit that does a work in our hearts. Genuine worship is powerful. Worship is not entertainment. Worship is not a distraction, like watching television. Worship is an encounter with God, and we are changed by that encounter. Reflecting upon his own experience, David says to the Lord in Psalm 30, 'You have turned for me my mourning into dancing; You have put off my sackcloth and clothed me with gladness.'

The End of the Wicked

 ¹⁸ Surely You set them in slippery places;
   You cast them down to destruction.
 ¹⁹ Oh, how they are brought to desolation, as in a moment!
   They are utterly consumed with terrors.

> ²⁰ **As a dream when one awakes, So, Lord, when You awake, You shall despise their image.**

In the sanctuary, Asaph began to view the wicked in a different light. He says, 'Then I understood their end'. The wicked seem to prosper, but where do they end up? What is the end of their story? What is the end of their lives? The psalmist learned that it is important not how we begin but how we end. The justice of God may come slowly, but it will come. God sets the wicked 'in slippery places.' Asaph said earlier that his feet almost slipped, but now he says it is the wicked who are slipping and sliding. Furthermore, God casts down the wicked 'to destruction', and in a moment they are utterly consumed.

The Psalmist Reflects upon the Experience

> ²¹ **Thus my heart was grieved,**
> **And I was vexed in my mind.**
> ²² **I was so foolish and ignorant;**
> **I was like a beast before You.**
> ²³ **Nevertheless I am continually with You;**
> **You hold me by my right hand.**
> ²⁴ **You will guide me with Your counsel,**
> **And afterward receive me to glory.**
> ²⁵ **Whom have I in heaven but You?**
> **And there is none upon earth that I desire besides You.**
> ²⁶ **My flesh and my heart fail;**
> **But God is the strength of my heart and**
> **my portion forever.**

Looking back on his experience, the psalmist grieves over his former attitude. He realizes that he had been 'foolish and ignorant'. He had envied the prosperity of the wicked; he had allowed discouragement to set in; and he had become depressed and bitter. He admits that his envy had caused him to start doing foolish things and speaking out in ignorance. He says to God, 'I was so foolish and ignorant, I was like a beast'. But God does not reject Asaph. God is 'continually' with him, holding his hand and guiding him into a brighter future. 'Afterward', the Lord will receive him 'to Glory'. The word 'afterward' is the same word as 'end'. When he went into the sanctuary, he learned the 'end' of the wicked. The end of the wicked is destruction, but the end of the righteous is glory.

Continuing to address God, the psalmist says, 'Whom have I in heaven but You? And there is none upon earth that I desire besides You.' God is guiding him, holding his right hand; therefore, what else does he need? At first, he had apparently desired to be prosperous like the wicked people whom he envied. Now, however, he desires only God. He desires to know God, to walk with God, and to be in the sanctuary of God. Even when his physical body breaks down, when his 'flesh and heart fail', God will be his strength and his 'portion'.

The Truth Appropriated in Life

²⁷ **For indeed, those who are far from You shall perish;**
 You have destroyed all those who desert You for harlotry.
²⁸ **But it is good for me to draw near to God;**
 I have put my trust in the Lord GOD,
 That I may declare all Your works.

Even though Asaph had seen the wicked prospering, he now concludes that all those who are 'far from' God 'shall perish'. God will destroy all those who are unfaithful and who desert God for 'harlotry'. Harlotry is a figure of speech that represents the forsaking of God for the worship of other gods, the worship of idols. Those who have forsaken God and have been unfaithful to God will be destroyed.

Asaph does not want to be one of those who is 'far' from God. He wants just the opposite – to be close to God. He says, 'It is good for me to draw near to God'. As he draws near to God, he will also put his 'trust in the Lord' and 'declare' all of God's works. The psalmist had earlier refused to speak, because he did not want to discourage other believers with his negative observations. Now, however, his heart overflows with a different kind of word, a word of praise. Now, his questions no longer are important. Now, he is able to talk of God's 'works'. He will tell what God has done, so that others can experience the same help that he experienced, so they can enjoy the same transformation that he has experienced. He will tell everyone what the Lord has done for him so that they also may be blessed. As we have said before, our blessings are not just for *us*, but God blesses *us* so that we can bless *others*. We bless others with our testimonies and by sharing what God has done.

Conclusion

Right in the middle of the book of Psalms, we have an example of the journey of faith. Psalm 73 begins with Asaph's trust in the goodness of God and his belief that evil is punished and good is rewarded. His initial theology is that of Psalm 1, in which the righteous are blessed and the wicked are doomed. But Asaph's theology is challenged by the inconsistencies that he observes around him. Just as we saw in Psalm 13 and 22, the psalmist notices that the righteous often suffer unjustly. God's people encounter troubles, while the wicked seem to prosper. In Psalm 73, Asaph moves from confidence in his hopeful theology into a period of doubt and discouragement. He then enters the sanctuary of God, where the Lord restores his faith and hope.

We learn from Psalm 73 that the truth will be challenged and that we will face serious questions. How will we handle the questions? – by entering the sanctuary of God. In worship, the clouds are scattered; our hearts are renewed; and hope is reborn.

Connecting with the Psalm

(Questions for discussion)

Have you ever struggled like Asaph regarding the prosperity of the wicked?

In light of Psalm 1, which teaches the prosperity of the righteous, how can we explain the prosperity of the wicked?

Explain the value of corporate worship as a transforming experience.

How does the Holy Spirit enhance our understanding of troubling questions?

Does Asaph receive an answer to his questions?

Does God always answer our questions?

What if … ?

(Creative and imaginative ideas)

What if we identify and list our most troubling questions?

What if we list the attributes of God that cause us to trust in him?

What if we prioritize worship and trust God to give us the answers that we need, when we need them?

What if we refrain from negative talk that would discourage our family members and other Christians?

Now, come up with your own 'What if … ?'

9

THE PASSIONATE PURSUIT OF PRAISE TO GOD: PSALM 150

Setting the Direction

God created us for a purpose. He made us so that we might worship him, serve him, and glorify him forever. He declared,

[You are] called by My name,
Whom I have created for My glory (Isa. 43.7).

Because we are created for God's glory, our pursuit of God must include the pursuit of praise to God. God has called us to praise him. He has saved us and chosen us as his people that we might praise him. He has formed us into the church of the living God in order that we may proclaim the praises of him who called us 'out of darkness into His marvelous light' (1 Pet. 2.9).

Life is a journey; and like Abraham, we travel to a place that we have never seen before. However, we do not wander aimlessly. We seek for the city 'whose builder and maker is God' (Heb. 11.10). We await the return of Jesus, and we look for the presence of God to come down out of heaven and for his kingdom to be established. God himself is the beginning and the end, and our goal is to reach the place of absolute praise.

More than any other psalm, Psalm 150 eloquently expresses our pursuit of praise to God. It is the only psalm that includes the word 'praise' in every line – 'praise' is encouraged thirteen times. This is the place of absolute praise to which God wants to bring us. This is the place of absolute praise that will bring fulfillment to our lives. This is the place of absolute praise that will bear witness to the fact that we are mature as Christians. This is the place of absolute praise that brings us into God's presence, whether it be at home, whether it be at church, or whether we be standing on the street corner. Absolute praise is when we can lift our voices to God, and we are not thinking about who we are or what our needs are; but we are thinking only of who God is and how wonderful it is to have him as the Lord of our lives. We lift up our voices to praise him and magnify him because of his greatness, because of his love, because of his mercy, because he is God and we are not God. We need to come to that place of mature praise where we can lift our voices to the Lord and say, 'O Lord, it is you, Lord. It is all about you. We come to worship you. O Lord, we are here to praise you, hallelujah! Lord, let us forget about ourselves, and our needs, and our circumstances, and let us just praise the name of the Lord.'

Psalm 150 exemplifies that kind of praise – total, absolute praise, where we are surrendered into the presence of God and where we worship him in Spirit and in Truth. Most of the world seeks for joy through entertainment, hobbies, and diversions. They go out to eat, watch a movie, go to the beach, play golf, hang out in clubs and bars, or watch TV. These leisure activities are ways of finding peace and joy in life. Many of these are helpful and acceptable, but they cannot replace worship; because it is in worship that we find our greatest fulfillment. We were created to worship God. We were created to have fellowship with God. We were created to know God, to love God, and to worship God with absolute praise. Psalm 150 expresses well our passionate pursuit of praise, and it serves as a fitting conclusion to the book of Psalms.

Discussion Starters

Explain the benefits of praising God.

Discuss the attributes of God for which you praise him.

What are your favorite kinds of music for worship?

Hearing the Word of God

Psalm 150

¹ Praise the LORD!
   Praise God in His sanctuary;
   Praise Him in His mighty firmament!
² Praise Him for His mighty acts;
   Praise Him according to His excellent greatness!
³ Praise Him with the sound of the trumpet;
   Praise Him with the lute and harp!
⁴ Praise Him with the timbrel and dance;
   Praise Him with stringed instruments and flutes!
⁵ Praise Him with loud cymbals;
   Praise Him with clashing cymbals!
⁶ Let everything that has breath praise the LORD.
   Praise the LORD!

The Songs of Praise

As we have said, Psalm 150 is one of the songs of praise (also called hymns). The songs of praise normally begin with an invitation to worship, followed by the reason or motive for praise, and end with a repeated invitation to worship. Note the following example from Psalms 135 and 113.

1. Call to Worship
   Praise the Lord; Praise the name of the Lord
   Praise him, O you servants of the Lord (135.1)
2. Motive for Worship
   A. God's Majesty
      (1) God's majesty in creation
         Whatever the Lord pleases, he does, In heaven and in earth,
         In the seas and in all the deep places (Ps. 135.6)
      (2) God's majesty in his sovereignty
         For I know that the Lord is great,
         And our Lord is above all gods (Ps. 135.5)
   B. God's Love
      (1) God's love in salvation (especially the exodus)
         He destroyed the firstborn of Egypt, Both of man and beast.

> *He sent signs and wonders* (Ps. 135.8-9)
> (2) God's love in provision and care
> *He raises the poor out of the dust,*
> *And lifts the needy out of the ash heap* (Ps. 113.7)

3. Concluding Call to Worship
> *Blessed be the Lord out of Zion, Who dwells in Jerusalem!*
> *Praise the Lord!* (Ps. 135.21)

The hymns teach us to praise God for his unchangeable attributes. He is the God who is majestic and exalted, the King of kings, the Lord of lords, the God of gods. He created the heaven, the earth, the angels, and all of humanity. So let us praise him! Not only is God majestic in his holiness, but he is also loving, kind, and compassionate. He saved Israel from the bondage of Egypt; therefore, let us praise him! The hymns teach us that the goal of worship is praise. When times are good, we should praise God; and when times are bad we should praise God.

Other hymns include Psalms 24, 29, 33, 46, 48, 50, 67, 68, 75, 76, 81, 82, 90, 100, 105, 107, 113, 114, 115, 117, 124, 125, 129, 134, 135, 136, 147, 149, and 150.

Praise the Lord …

Psalm 150 can be divided into five parts:

1. Invitation to praise (v. 1a) (Call to Worship)
2. Places for praise (v. 1b)
3. Motivation for praise (v. 2) (Motive for Worship)
4. Methods of praise (vv. 3-5)
5. Universal praise (v. 6) (Concluding Call to Worship)

Invitation to Praise

[1a] Praise the LORD!

Psalm 150 begins with an invitation to the congregation, 'Praise the LORD!'. The Hebrew word 'praise' is the imperative form of the verb, which suggests a command or an urgent exhortation. 'Praise the LORD!' is a call to worship, urging the entire congregation to participate in the praise of the Lord. No one should be a spectator – everyone should praise him.

Who is the object of our praise? The Lord! Who is the Lord? The Lord is Yahweh (traditionally known as Jehovah). He is the God of Abraham, Isaac, and Jacob. He is the God who met Moses at the burning bush in Exodus 3. He said, 'Moses, I have come down to deliver my people Israel, to deliver them from the bondage of Egypt and out of the house of slavery and to lead them into a land that flows with milk and honey, the land I promised unto Abraham'. Yahweh is the God who brought Israel out of bondage, out of slavery. He is Jehovah-Jireh (Gen. 22.14), the Lord who provides. He is Jehovah-Ropheh, the Lord who heals us (Exod. 15.26). He is Jehovah-Shalom, the Lord our peace (Ps. 6.24). He is Jehovah-Tsidkenu, the Lord our righteousness (Jer. 23.6). He is Jehovah-Nissi, the Lord our banner (Exod. 17.15). He is Yahweh. He is Jehovah. The psalmist did not say praise Allah, or praise Buddha, or praise Krishna – he said, 'praise the LORD'. We are invited to come and praise him.

Places of Praise

**¹ᵇ Praise God in His sanctuary;
Praise Him in His mighty firmament!**

The second element of verse 1 tells us where we should praise him. First, we should 'Praise God in His sanctuary'. His 'sanctuary' means his 'holy place'. Here in Psalm 150, the sanctuary probably refers to two locations: God's heavenly abode and his dwelling place in the Jerusalem temple. Therefore, all of the heavenly servants should praise God in heaven, and all of the earthly servants should praise God in the temple. Also, our churches are buildings that are dedicated as a place of worship unto the Lord. Therefore, the church facility is a holy place, a sanctuary that is devoted to God's use. Jesus taught us that where any two or three are gathered together in his name, he is in the midst of them. Wherever Jesus is present, it is a holy place. Wherever God's holy people are gathered together, that is a holy place. It is all about God and his people.

The psalmist goes beyond the sanctuary and says, 'Praise him in his mighty firmament'. In order to understand the word 'firmament', we must go back to Genesis, where we read,

> And God said, Let there be a firmament in the midst of the waters, and let it divide the waters from the waters. And God made the firmament, and divided the waters which were under the

firmament from the waters which were above the firmament: and it was so. And God called the firmament Heaven. And the evening and the morning were the second day (Gen. 1.6-8).

On the second day of creation, God divided the waters that were on the surface of the earth (oceans, rivers, and lakes) from the waters that are above the earth (clouds). Clouds are nothing but water vapor, and between the clouds and the earth is the open sky, which Genesis calls 'the firmament'. It imagines that there is a dome above the sky which holds back the clouds. The sky separates the earth from the clouds. So when he says, 'Praise Him in his mighty firmament', he means, 'Praise Him beneath the sky'. Wherever we are upon the earth and are able to look up and see the sky, the stars, the sun, the moon, and the clouds, that is a place in which we should praise the Lord. We know that heaven is filled with praise, and heaven lies beyond the firmament, beyond the sky. In Psalm 150, we are told that inside the firmament, inside the circle of the sky, we are to praise God. Whenever we look up and see the stars, let us remember the earlier words of the psalmist: 'The heavens declare the glory of God, and the firmament shows forth His handiwork' (Ps. 19.1). Any time we are under the sky, we are in a place of praise. He created the sky with the power of his word, so let us praise him!

Motivation for Praise

² **Praise Him for His mighty acts;**
Praise Him according to His excellent greatness!

The third section of this psalm expresses the motive for praise: 'Praise Him for His mighty acts; Praise Him for His excellent greatness'. Yahweh is the God who works and acts on our behalf. He intervenes in our lives. Some people think that God created all things and then stood back to let the world run on its own, but God is very much involved in the world and our lives. Therefore, we come to God in prayer, bringing our needs to the Lord; and we come before God in worship, pouring out our hearts to the Lord. The Lord is involved in meeting our needs, hearing our prayers, working miracles, directing our steps, and delivering us daily. 'Praise Him for His mighty acts'. God is neither impotent nor lazy. God is neither detached nor unconcerned. He is powerful and active, and he cares deeply about his people.

The psalmist then says that we should praise God for his attributes: 'Praise Him according to His excellent greatness'. Why should we praise God? Because 'Great is the LORD and greatly to be praised' (Ps. 145.3). Praise him because he is great in wisdom. Praise him because he is great in holiness. Praise him because he is great in power. Praise him because he is great in love. Praise him because he is great in faithfulness. Praise him because he is great in his mercy.

Methods of Praise

> ³ **Praise Him with the sound of the trumpet;**
>   **Praise Him with the lute and harp!**
> ⁴ **Praise Him with the timbrel and dance;**
>   **Praise Him with stringed instruments and flutes!**
> ⁵ **Praise Him with loud cymbals;**
>   **Praise Him with clashing cymbals!**

The fourth section of the psalm lists the various methods of worship or ways of worship. The psalmist insists that every musical instrument should be used to praise the Lord. Unlike humans, who have preferences for certain musical instruments, God loves to hear every musical instrument that is used in praising him. The psalmist lists all three kinds of musical instruments: percussion instruments, wind instruments, and stringed instruments. The wind instruments are the trumpets and the pipes. The stringed instruments are the psaltery and the harp. The percussion instruments are the timbrel (tambourine) and the cymbals. He then goes beyond instruments to include the dance. It was common in those days to dance while playing a tambourine. Those of us who cannot play musical instruments can dance in praise unto the Lord. Other physical modes of worship are mentioned in earlier psalms, such as the clapping of hands and shouting.

Our worship services are not meant to be entertainment; they are meant to be offerings unto God. Therefore, our music should be directed toward the Lord as a sacrifice of praise. The New Testament describes our worship as a 'sacrifice of praise': 'By him therefore let us offer the sacrifice of praise to God continually, that is, the fruit of our lips giving thanks to his name' (Heb. 13.15). Our participation in worship, whether it be by playing an instrument, clapping our hands, singing, or shouting, should be an offering to the Lord.

Universal Praise

> ⁶ **Let everything that has breath praise the LORD.**
> **Praise the LORD!**

Finally, the psalmist tells us that all people should praise God. The invitation to praise is not directed only to the pastor: 'All of you pastors, praise the Lord'. This invitation to praise is not meant only for church leaders, singers, or the worship team. This invitation is directed at everyone: 'Let everything that has breath praise the LORD'. Scripture tells us that God breathed into Adam the breath of life (Gen. 2.7) and that God gives breath to every person (Acts 17.25). Let us use that breath to praise God – 'Let everything that has breath praise the Lord'.

The Hebrew text of Ps. 150.6 says literally, 'Let every breath praise Yahweh'. God has given us our breath, and with our breath he gave us the freedom to choose how to use that breath. We can breathe forth blessing or we can breathe forth cursing. We can use our breath to bless God, or we can use our breath to curse God. We can use our breath to injure or to heal, to hurt or to help. We have the choice of how we use our breath. Psalm 150 invites us to use our breath in absolute praise! As God breathes into us, we inhale; then as we exhale, let it be praise. Every breath that goes forth from our mouth should be praise. Let us not breathe out hatred; let us not breathe out hurt; let us not breathe out injury; let us not breathe out envy; let us not breathe forth strife; let us not breathe forth profanity; let us not breathe forth cursing. Rather, let us breathe forth blessing. Let us breathe forth honor. Let us breathe forth praise to the Lord. Let everything that has breath praise the Lord. Let us pray as David prayed, 'Let the words of my mouth and the meditations of my heart be acceptable in thy sight, O Lord, my strength and my Redeemer' (Ps. 19.14). Praise ye the Lord. Praise his holy name.

If we look back to Psalm 148, we will find more detail about God's desire for universal praise. The psalmist says,

> ² Praise Him, all His angels;
>   Praise Him, all His hosts!
> ³ Praise Him, sun and moon;
>   Praise Him, all you stars of light!
> ⁴ Praise Him, you heavens of heavens,

And you waters above the heavens!
⁵ Let them praise the name of the LORD,
   For He commanded and they were created.
⁶ He also established them forever and ever;
   He made a decree which shall not pass away.
⁷ Praise the LORD from the earth,
   You great sea creatures and all the depths;
⁸ Fire and hail, snow and clouds;
   Stormy wind, fulfilling His word;
⁹ Mountains and all hills;
   Fruitful trees and all cedars;
¹⁰ Beasts and all cattle;
   Creeping things and flying fowl;
¹¹ Kings of the earth and all peoples;
   Princes and all judges of the earth;
¹² Both young men and maidens;
   Old men and children.
¹³ Let them praise the name of the LORD, (Ps. 148.2-13).

Praise is not an option for us. We must praise him when things are going well, and we must praise him when things are falling apart. We must praise him when we feel like it, and we must praise him when we do not feel like it.

Psalm 150 concludes with a powerful statement of absolute praise. We must come to the place where we can focus entirely upon God and upon giving him praise. We must forget everything else. If we read through the Psalms, we will find plenty of reasons for coming to God with absolute praise.

- We have heard that the Lord is our shepherd, and we shall not want; so let us praise him.

- We have read that he is our rock and our fortress, so let us praise him.

- We have heard that the heavens declare the glory of God, so let us praise him.

- We have heard that the earth is the Lord's and the fullness thereof, so let us praise him.

- We heard that the Lord is our light and our salvation, so let us praise him.

- We heard that the Lord brought us up out of a horrible pit, so let us praise him.
- We heard that the Lord is our refuge and strength, a very present help in a time of need; so let us praise him.
- We have heard that the Lord is good, his mercy is everlasting, and his truth endures to all generations; so let us praise him.
- We have heard that he has forgiven all of our sins, so let us praise him.
- We also read that he heals all of our diseases, so let us praise him.
- We have heard that his greatness is unsearchable, so let us praise him.
- We have heard that he will reign as king forever and forever, so let us praise him.
- We heard that the Lord is coming, so let us praise him.
- Let us praise him, not because of a specific answer to prayer, but because of who he is.
- Let us praise him, not because of just one event when he came to our rescue, but because he is God.
- Let us praise him because he is Savior, sanctifier, Spirit baptizer, healer, and coming king.
- Let us praise him because he is worthy to open the book (Rev. 5.2-5).
- Praise him because he is King of Kings and Lord of lords.
- Praise him because he is the Alpha and the Omega.
- Praise him because he is the Lamb of God who takes away the sins of the world.
- Praise him because he dwells in the midst of his people.
- Praise him because he is a father to the orphan and a husband to the widow.
- Praise him because he supplies all of our need.
- Praise him for his mighty acts; praise him according to his excellent greatness.
- Let every breath praise the Lord!

The Message of the Book of Psalms

The book of Psalms is relevant to every point in our journey of faith. Our every experience finds correspondence either in the praises, the prayers, or the teachings of the book of Psalms. The entire span of worship is encapsulated here in Israel's songbook. In this book of praises, we also find songs of lament and songs of teaching. Every part of the life of faith is explored in the Psalms.

The book of Psalms begins by pronouncing blessings upon the righteous person who delights in the 'law of the LORD' and meditates in it 'day and night'. That person is like a tree planted by the rivers of water that brings forth its fruit in its season, and whatsoever he does will prosper. But the wicked are not so. The wicked are like the husk of the grain that the wind blows away. The wicked cannot stand in the day of judgment, and they do not have a place in the congregation of the righteous. Psalm one concludes by saying that the Lord knows the way of the righteous, but the way of the ungodly will perish.

We begin the book of Psalms, therefore, with a contrast between the righteous and the wicked. The righteous person loves to worship God, and God blesses the worshiper. We do not receive the blessings of God by seeking our own way, by seeking after the things of the world. Jesus said, 'Seek first the kingdom of God and his righteousness, and all of these things will be added to you' (Mt. 6.33). We are blessed when we seek the Word of God, the worship of God, and the praise of God. We must come to God with our whole heart to worship him, to meditate in his word, and to walk in his way. If we do this, God will bless us, and he will prosper us.

However, when we get to Psalm 3, we learn that righteous people do not always have it easy. They often encounter opposition in various forms. Therefore, we find psalms of urgent prayer, which we call laments, in which the righteous person cries out to God. In Psalm 13 David prays, 'How long? Oh LORD, would you forget me forever? How long, O LORD, will you let me suffer? How long will I endure this pain in my soul?'

These psalms of lament remind us of the story of Job. Even a righteous person like Job – who is perfect, upright, fearing God, and shunning evil – will suffer. He was a righteous man, yet God allowed a testing time in his life. The Psalms show us that during times of testing the psalmist would cry out to God and plead for God's help.

We also go through those kinds of experiences. When we are in the midst of the valley, the way to get out of the valley is to bow our knees before the Lord, pour out our hearts to God, and worship him wholeheartedly. We must not ignore God when we are in the valley. Furthermore, we must not avoid the church when we are suffering. Many people make the mistake of trying to face their problems alone. When we are in trouble, that is when we really need the church. The church is where we can pray. The church is where brothers and sisters will intercede for us. We need one another when we are in trouble, and we must not shut out people when we are in need.

In our times of trouble we can go to the Psalms and find examples of how we should seek the face of God. What happens when we pray? God answers. In answer to our prayers, God sends blessings. In answer to our prayers, God sends healings. In answer to our prayers, God sends miracles. As we read through the Psalms, we find prayers; then we find psalms of thanksgiving.

In the psalms of thanksgiving, the psalmist gives thanks to God for his answers to prayer. An example of the psalm of thanksgiving is Psalm 40, in which the psalmist testifies of God's saving power. He 'cried unto the LORD' in the midst of his trouble, and God 'inclined' to him and heard his cry. God bent down to listen; then, he lifted him up out of the horrible pit, out of the mirey clay, and he set his feet upon a rock. We could also point to Psalm 107, in which those who wandered in the wilderness cried unto the Lord, and the Lord heard their cry and delivered them from all their troubles. Therefore, we should 'praise the LORD for his goodness and for his wonderful works unto the children of men' (Ps. 107.8). Those who were sick and afflicted cried to God, and God sent his word and healed them. Therefore, we should praise him.

So the book of Psalms begins with a call to righteousness and worship. Then it moves on to the psalms of prayer, in which the psalmist relates a time of deep suffering and pain. Out of that pain, the psalmist cries to God for help. When God answers the psalmist's prayers, a song of thanksgiving is offered. In addition to the praises that are offered in response to a specific time of deliverance, the book of Psalms records hymns of praise that exalt the Lord for his nature and attributes.

This progression, however, is not a simple step-by-step process that always begins with teaching, leads to prayer, and ends in praise. Psalm 40, for example, begins with praise and ends with prayer. The life of faith is not the same every day. The Christian life is not all sorrow, and it is not all joy. We go through trials of our faith, tests, opposition, and troubles. Yet, the Christian life is not all testing and trouble – God gives us deliverance and God gives us joy. As the psalmist said, 'Weeping may endure for a night, but joy comes in the morning' (Ps. 30.5).

The book of Psalms concludes with a series of four hymns of praise. These last four psalms bring us to a whole new level of praise. Psalms 147-150 encourage us to praise God for his character and his attributes. These last few psalms might be called psalms of absolute praise. In the hymns of praise, the focus of the attention is no longer on our prayers and how God answered us; but the emphasis is upon God, his nature, his holiness, his power, his majesty, his love, and his grace. The praise is focused entirely upon God and his nature and purposes and work.

Absolute praise

Psalm 150 is the greatest example of absolute praise, and its placement at the end of the Psalter points to the fact that our goal as God's people is to worship God completely. As we journey with God, we live before him, pray unto him and give our give thanks to him. We experience the ups and downs of life and sometimes seem to be going nowhere. However, Psalm 150 teaches us that we have one goal, and we are headed in one direction – our goal is the place of absolute praise. One day, every knee will bow before him, and every tongue will confess that Jesus Christ is Lord, to the glory of God the father (Phil. 2.10-11). We are moving towards the day when everything in heaven will praise God, everything in the earth will praise God, and everything under the earth will praise the name of the Lord. Every part of creation will give praise and glory to God (Rev. 5.11-14). Our goal is a time and a place where there will be no more sun, because the Son of God will be the light. And God's city, the holy city, new Jerusalem, will come down from God out of heaven; and the city will be in the midst of his people, and God will dwell in the midst of us;

he will be the temple. We will live and remain in his presence to glorify and praise him for ever and ever.

Praise is our goal

In the New Testament, we are called to absolute praise by the Apostle Paul who writes, 'Rejoice in the Lord always. Again I will say, rejoice!' (Phil. 4.4), and 'to him be glory in the church … forever and ever'(Eph. 3.21). John envisioned a day when God's people would be enveloped in absolute praise. He writes,

> After these things I looked, and behold, a great multitude which no one could number, of all nations, tribes, peoples, and tongues, standing before the throne and before the Lamb, clothed with white robes, with palm branches in their hands, and crying out with a loud voice, saying, 'Salvation belongs to our God who sits on the throne, and to the Lamb!' All the angels stood around the throne and the elders and the four living creatures, and fell on their faces before the throne and worshiped God, saying: 'Amen! Blessing and glory and wisdom, thanksgiving and honor and power and might, be to our God forever and ever. Amen (Rev. 7.9-12).

There is no difference in status or rank among the heavenly multitude in Revelation 7. Every person has equal access to the presence of God. One is not better than the other, but all are standing before the throne of God with palm branches in their hands and the praises of God on their lips. This is the kind of praise to which Psalm 150 calls us. We must pattern our worship after the worship of heaven. We must come to the place where we forget ourselves and get lost in his praises. We must become immersed in praise like David, who 'danced before the LORD with all his might' (2 Sam. 6.14) and like John who 'was in the Spirit on the LORD's day' (Rev. 1.10).

Connecting with the Psalm

(Questions for discussion)

Discuss the places where we should engage in praise to God.

Are certain musical instruments more appropriate for worship than other instruments?

What are the elements of acceptable worship according to Psalm 150?

How does our culture contribute to the kind of worship that we employ?

Discuss the phrase, 'His excellent greatness' (v. 2).

Why is it essential that we pursue the passionate praise of God?

What if ... ?

(Creative and imaginative ideas)

What if we create a plan to include more musical instruments in our worship?

What if we encourage the youth to be involved in the church's music program?

What if we set aside time every day to give praise to God?

Now, come up with your own 'What if ... ?'

REFERENCES

BDB: Brown, Francis *et al.*, *The New Brown, Driver, Briggs, Gesenius Hebrew and English Lexicon: With an Appendix Containing the Biblical Aramaic* (trans. Edward Robinson; Peabody, MA: Hendrickson, 1979).

Blumhofer, Edith Waldvogel, *'Pentecost in My Soul': Explorations in the Meaning of Pentecostal Experience in the Assemblies of God* (Springfield, MO: Gospel Pub. House, 1989).

Clines, David J.A. (ed.), *The Concise Dictionary of Classical Hebrew* (Sheffield, UK: Sheffield Phoenix Press, 2009).

Dahood, Mitchell J., *Psalms* (Anchor Bible; 3 vols.; Garden City, NY: Doubleday, 1966).

Land, Steven Jack, *Pentecostal Spirituality: A Passion for the Kingdom* (Cleveland, TN: CPT Press, 2010).

TWOT: Harris, R. Laird, Gleason Leonard Archer, and Bruce K. Waltke, *Theological Wordbook of the Old Testament* (2 vols.; Chicago: Moody Press, 1980).

RESOURCES FOR FURTHER STUDY

Brueggemann, Walter, *The Message of the Psalms : A Theological Commentary* (Augsburg Old Testament Studies; Minneapolis: Augsburg Pub. House, 1984).

Bullock, C. Hassell, *Encountering the Book of Psalms : A Literary and Theological Introduction* (Encountering Biblical Studies; Grand Rapids, MI: Baker Academic, 2001).

Goldingay, John, *Psalms* (Baker Commentary on the Old Testament Wisdom and Psalms; 3 vols.; Grand Rapids, MI: Baker Academic, 2006).

Martin, Lee Roy, *The Spirit of the Psalms* (Cleveland, TN: CPT Press, 2018).

Mays, James Luther, *Psalms* (Interpretation; Louisville, KY: John Knox Press, 1994).

Wilcock, Michael, *The Message of Psalms: Songs for the People of God* (Bible Speaks Today; 2 vols.; Downers Grove, IL: InterVarsity Press, 2001).

INDEX OF BIBLICAL REFERENCES

Made in the USA
Columbia, SC
03 March 2023

13294147R00104